Primitive Athens
as described by Thucydides

Primitive Athens
as described by Thucydides

by

JANE ELLEN HARRISON,

HON. D.LITT. (DURHAM), HON. LL.D. (ABERDEEN),
STAFF LECTURER AND SOMETIME FELLOW OF NEWNHAM COLLEGE, CAMBRIDGE.

Cambridge
at the University Press
1906

CAMBRIDGE
UNIVERSITY PRESS

University Printing House, Cambridge CB2 8BS, United Kingdom

Published in the United States of America by Cambridge University Press, New York

Cambridge University Press is part of the University of Cambridge.

It furthers the University's mission by disseminating knowledge in the pursuit of education, learning and research at the highest international levels of excellence.

www.cambridge.org
Information on this title: www.cambridge.org/9781107644243

First published 1906
First paperback edition 2014

A catalogue record for this publication is available from the British Library

ISBN 978-1-107-64424-3 Paperback

VILHELMO DOERPFELD

HUNC QUALEMCUNQUE LIBELLUM

ANIMO SALTEM NON INGRATO

DEDICAT

J. E. H.

Πηγὴν μὲν πολύκρουνον Ἀθηναίης ἀνέφηνας
πηγὴ δ᾽ αὐτὸς ἔφυς καλλιρόου σοφίης.

PREFACE.

MY *Mythology and Monuments of Ancient Athens* has been for some time out of print. I have decided to issue no second edition. A word of explanation is therefore needed as to the purport of the present pages.

Since my book on Athens was published Dr Frazer's great commentary on Pausanias has appeared, and for scholars has made a second edition, so far as my book was a commentary on Pausanias, superfluous. The need for a popular handbook has been met by Professor Ernest Gardner's *Ancient Athens*. It happens however that, on a question cardinal for the understanding of the early history of Athens, I hold views diametrically opposed to both these writers. These views I have felt bound to state.

This cardinal question is the interpretation of an account given by Thucydides of the character and limits of ancient Athens. Both Dr Frazer and Professor Ernest Gardner hold by an interpretation which though almost universally prevalent down to recent times has been, in my opinion, disproved by the recent excavations of the German Archaeological Institute at Athens and the explanation of their results by Professor Dörpfeld. An adequate examination of the new theory could perhaps hardly be expected in such a book as Professor Gardner's, and it will not be found there. Dr Frazer, it is needless to say, stated Professor Dörpfeld's view with fulness and fairness, so far as was then possible or consistent with his main purpose. But the passage of Thucydides deserves and requires a more full consideration than it could receive incidentally in an edition of

Pausanias. Moreover at the time when Dr Frazer visited Athens the excavations were only in process, and the results had not been fully developed when his book was published. It was therefore impossible for Dr Frazer to give in one place such a connected account of the new evidence and theory as in a question of this magnitude seems desirable.

The view I set forth is not my own but that of Professor Dörpfeld. In the light of his examination of the passage of Thucydides what had been a mere 'Enneakrounos Episode' interesting only to specialists, became at once a vital question affecting the whole history of primitive Athens. Professor Dörpfeld's views convinced me even before they were confirmed by excavation. I expressed my adhesion in my *Mythology and Monuments of Ancient Athens*, but I did not then see their full significance. For English readers these views have been so far stated as heresies to be combated, or as rash speculations needing danger-signals. The danger seems to me the other way. To my mind this is a case where adherence to traditional views can only leave us in straits made desperate by the advancing tide of knowledge. I have therefore set forth Prof. Dörpfeld's views, not apologetically, but in full confidence, as illuminating truths essentially conciliatory and constructive.

Save in the Conclusion, on the question of the *metastasis*, I have added to the topographical argument nothing of my own. If here and there I have been unable to resist the temptation of wandering into bye-paths of religion and mythology, I trust the reader will pardon one who is by nature no topographer. For topography all that I have done is to set forth as clearly and fully as I could a somewhat intricate argument.

This task—not very easy because alien to my own present work—has been lightened by the help of many friends. Professor Dörpfeld has found time while excavating at Pergamos to go over my proofs and to assure me that his views are correctly represented. The German Archaeological Institute has generously placed at my disposal the whole of their official publications, from which my illustrations are mainly drawn. The like facilities in the matter of the Acropolis excavations have been kindly accorded me by Dr Kabbadias. Other sources are noted in their place. In the matter of re-drawing, in restorations and the modification of plans I have again to thank Mrs Hugh Stewart for much difficult and delicate work, work which could only be done by one who is archaeologist as well as artist.

My debt, by now habitual, to Dr Verrall will appear throughout the book. Mr Gilbert Murray has written for me the Critical Note and has made many fruitful suggestions. Mr F. M. Cornford has helped me throughout, and has revised the whole of my proofs. And last, for any degree of accuracy that may have been attained in the printing, I am indebted to the skill and care of the University Press.

JANE ELLEN HARRISON.

Newnham College, Cambridge.
18 *January*, 1906.

TABLE OF CONTENTS.

CHAPTER IV.

THE SPRING KALLIRRHOË-ENNEAKROUNOS 'NEAR' THE CITADEL.

INTRODUCTORY.

THE traveller who visits Athens for the first time will naturally, if he be a classical scholar, devote himself at the outset to the realization of the city of Perikles. His task will here be beset by no serious difficulties. The Acropolis, as Perikles left it, is, both from literary and monumental evidence, adequately known to us. Archaeological investigation has now but little to add to the familiar picture, and that little in matters of quite subordinate detail. The Parthenon, the Propylaea, the temple of Nike Apteros, the Erechtheion (this last probably planned, though certainly not executed by Perikles) still remain to us; their ground-plans and their restorations are for the most part architectural certainties. Moreover, even outside the Acropolis, the situation and limits of the city of Perikles are fairly well ascertained. The Acropolis itself was, we know, a fortified sanctuary within a larger walled city. This city lay, as the oracle in Herodotus[1] said, 'wheel-shaped' about the axle of the sacred hill. Portions of this outside wall have come to light here and there, and the foundations of the great Dipylon Gate are clearly made out, and are marked in every guide-book. Inside the circuit of these walls, in the inner Kerameikos, whose boundary-stone still remains, lay the agora. Outside is still to be seen, with its street of tombs, the ancient cemetery.

Should the sympathies of the scholar extend to Roman times, he has still, for the making of his mental picture, all the help imagination needs. Through the twisted streets of modern Athens the beautiful Tower of the Winds is his constant land-mark; Hadrian, with his Olympieion, with his triumphal Arch, with his Library, confronts him at every turn; when he goes to the great

---

[1] Herod. VII. 140.

Stadion to see 'Olympian' games or a revived 'Antigone,' when
he looks down from the Acropolis into the vast Odeion, Herodes
Atticus cannot well be forgotten.   Moreover, if he really cares to
know what Athens was in Roman days, the scholar can leave
behind him his Murray and his Baedeker and take for his only
guide the contemporary of Hadrian, Pausanias.

But returning, as he inevitably will, again and again to the
Acropolis, the scholar will gradually become conscious, if dimly,
of another and an earlier Athens.   On his plan of the Acropolis
he will find marked certain fragments of very early masonry,
which, he is told, are 'Pelasgian.'   As he passes to the south
of the Parthenon he comes upon deep-sunk pits railed in, and
within them he can see traces of these 'Pelasgian' walls and other
masonry about which his guide-book is not over-explicit.   To the
south of the Propylaea, to his considerable satisfaction, he comes
on a solid piece of this 'Pelasgian' wall, still above ground.   East
of the Erechtheion he will see a rock-hewn stair-way which once,
he learns, led down from the palace of the ancient prehistoric
kings, the 'strong house of Erechtheus.'   South of the Erechtheion
he can make out with some effort the ground plan of an early
temple ; he is told that there exist bases of columns belonging to
a yet earlier structure, and these he probably fails to find.

With all his efforts he can frame but a hazy picture of this
earlier Acropolis, this citadel before the Persian wars.   Probably
he might drop the whole question as of merely antiquarian interest—a matter to be noted rather than realized—but that his
next experience brings sudden revelation.   Skilfully sunk out
of sight—to avoid interfering with his realization of Periklean
Athens—is the small Acropolis Museum.   Entering it, he finds
himself in a moment actually within that other and earlier Athens
dimly discerned, and instantly he knows it, not as a world of
ground-plans and fragmentary Pelasgic fortifications, but as a
kingdom of art and of humanity vivid with colour and beauty.

As he passes in eager excitement through the ante-rooms he
will glance, as he goes, at the great blue lion and the bull, at the
tangle of rampant many-coloured snakes, at the long-winged birds
with their prey still in beak and talon ; he will pause to smile
back at the three kindly 'Bluebeards,' he will be glad when
he sees that the familiar Calf-Carrier has found his feet and

his name, he will note the long rows of solemn votive terra-cottas, and, at last, he will stand in the presence of those Maiden-images, who, amid all that coloured architectural splendour, were consecrate to the worship of the Maiden. The Persian harried them, Perikles left them to lie beneath his feet, yet their antique loveliness is untouched and still sovran. They are alive, waiting still, in hushed, intent expectancy—but not for us. We go out from their presence as from a sanctuary, and henceforth every stone of the Pelasgian fortress where they dwelt is, for us, sacred.

But if he leave that museum aglow with a new enthusiasm, determined to know what is to be known of that antique world, the scholar will assuredly be met on the threshold of his enquiry by difficulties and disillusionment. By difficulties, because the information he seeks is scattered through a mass of foreign periodical literature, German and Greek; by disillusionment, because to the simple questions he wants to ask he can get no clear, straightforward answer. He wants to know what was the nature and extent of the ancient city, did it spread beyond the Acropolis, if so in what direction and how far? what were the primitive sanctuaries inside the Pelasgic walls, what, if any, lay outside and where? Where was the ancient city well (Kallirrhoe), where the agora, where that primitive orchestra on which, before the great theatre was built, dramatic contests took place? Straightway he finds himself plunged into a very cauldron of controversy. The ancient agora is placed by some to the north, by others to the south, by others again to the west. The question of its position is inextricably bound up, he finds to his surprise, with the question as to where lay the Enneakrounos, a fountain with which hitherto he has had no excessive familiarity; the mere mention of the Enneakrounos brings either a heated discussion or, worse, a chilling silence.

This atmosphere of controversy, electric with personal prejudice, exhilarating as it is to the professed archaeologist, plunges the scholar in a profound dejection. His concern is not *jurare in verba magistri*—he wants to know not *who* but *what* is right. Two questions only he asks. First, and perhaps to him unduly foremost, What, as to the primitive city, is the literary testimony of the ancients themselves, and preferably the testimony not of scholiasts and second-hand lexicographers, but of classical writers who knew and lived in Athens, of Thucydides, of Pausanias ? Second, To that literary testimony, what of monumental evidence has been added by excavation ?

It is to answer these two questions that the following pages are written. It is the present writer's conviction that controversy as to the main outlines of the picture, though perhaps at the outset inevitable, is, with the material now accessible, an anachronism; that the facts stand out plain and clear and that between the literary and monumental evidence there is no discrepancy. The plan adopted will therefore be to state as simply as may be what seems the ascertained truth about the ancient city, and to state that truth unencumbered by controversy. Then, and not till then, it may be profitable to mention other current opinions, and to examine briefly what seem to be the errors in method which have led to their acceptance.

CHAPTER I.

THE ANCIENT CITY, ITS CHARACTER AND LIMITS.

By a rare good fortune we have from Thucydides himself an account of the nature and extent of the city of Athens in the time of the kingship. This account is not indeed as explicit in detail as we could wish, but in general outline it is clear and vivid. To the scholar the remembrance of this account comes as a ray of light in his darkness. If he cannot find his way in the mazes of archaeological controversy, it is at least his business to read Thucydides and his hope to understand him.

The account of primitive Athens is incidental. Thucydides is telling how, during the Peloponnesian War, when the enemy was mustering on the Isthmus and attack on Attica seemed imminent, Perikles advised the Athenians to desert their country homes and take refuge in the city. The Athenians were convinced by his arguments. They sent their sheep and cattle to Euboea and the islands; they pulled down even the wood-work of their houses, and themselves, with their wives, their children, and all their moveable property, migrated to Athens. But, says Thucydides[1], this 'flitting' went hard with them; and why? Because 'they had always, most of them, been used to a country life.'

This habit of 'living in the fields,' this country life was, Thucydides goes on to explain, no affair of yesterday; it had been so from the earliest times. All through the days of the kingship from Kekrops to Theseus the people had lived scattered about in small communities—'village communities' we expect to hear him say, for he is insisting on the habit of country life; but, though he knows the word 'village' (κώμη) and employs it in discussing

---

[1] Thucyd. II. 14 χαλεπῶς δὲ αὐτοῖς, διὰ τὸ ἀεὶ εἰωθέναι τοὺς πολλοὺς ἐν τοῖς ἀγροῖς διαιτᾶσθαι, ἡ ἀνάστασις ἐγίγνετο.

Laconia elsewhere[1], he does not use it here. He says the inhabitants of Athens lived 'in towns' (κατὰ πόλεις), or, as it would be safer to translate it, 'in burghs.'

It is necessary at the outset to understand clearly what the word *polis* here means. We use the word 'town' in contradistinction to country, but from the account of Thucydides it is clear that people could live in a *polis* and yet lead a country life. Our word *city* is still less appropriate; 'city' to us means a very large town, a place where people live crowded together. A *polis*, as Thucydides here uses the word, was a community of people living on and immediately about a fortified hill or citadel— a citadel-community. The life lived in such a community was essentially a country life. A *polis* was a citadel, only that our word 'citadel' is over-weighted with military association.

Athens then, in the days of Kekrops and the other kings down to Theseus, was one among many other citadel-communities or burghs. Like the other scattered burghs, like Aphidna, like Thoricus, like Eleusis, it had its own local government, its own council-house, its own magistrates. So independent were these citadel-communities that, Thucydides tells us, on one occasion Eleusis under Eumolpos actually made war on Athens under Erechtheus.

So things went on till the reign of Theseus and his famous Synoikismos, the Dwelling-together or Unification. Theseus, Thucydides says, was a man of ideas and of the force of character necessary to carry them out. He substituted the one for the many; he put an end to the little local councils and council-houses and centralized the government of Attica in Athens. Where the government is, thither naturally population will flock. People began to gather into Athens, and for a certain percentage of the population town-life became fashionable. Then, and not till then, did the city become 'great,' and that 'great' city Theseus handed down to posterity. 'And from that time down to the present day the Athenians celebrate to the Goddess at the public expense a festival called the Dwelling-together[2].'

One unified city and one goddess, *the goddess* who needs no

---

[1] Thucyd. I. 5, 10.

[2] Thucyd. II. 15 καὶ ξυνοίκια ἐξ ἐκείνου Ἀθηναῖοι ἔτι καὶ νῦν τῇ θεῷ ἑορτὴν δημοτελῆ ποιοῦσι.

name. Their unity and their greatness the Athenians are not
likely to forget, but will they remember the time before the
union, when Athens was but Kekropia, but one among the many
scattered citadel-communities? Will they remember how small
was their own beginning, how limited their burgh, how impossible—for that is the immediate point—that it should have
contained in its narrow circuit a large town population? Thucydides clearly is afraid they will *not*. There was much to prevent
accurate realization. The walls of Themistocles, when Thucydides
wrote, enclosed a *polis* that was not very much smaller than the
modern town; the walls of the earlier community, the old small
burgh, were in part ruined. It was necessary therefore, if the
historian would make clear his point, namely, the smallness of
the ancient burgh and its inadequacy for town-life, that he should
define its limits. This straightway he proceeds to do. Our whole
discussion will centre round his definition and description, and at
the outset the passage must be given in full. Immediately after
his notice of the festival of the ' Dwelling-together,' celebrated to
' the Goddess,' Thucydides[1] writes as follows:

> *Before this, what is now the citadel was the city, together with
> what is below it towards about south. The evidence is this. The
> sanctuaries are in the citadel itself, those of other deities as well*[2] *(as
> the Goddess). And those that are outside are placed towards this
> part of the city more (than elsewhere). Such are the sanctuary of
> Zeus Olympios, and the Pythion, and the sanctuary of Ge, and that
> of Dionysos-in-the-Marshes (to whom is celebrated the more ancient
> Dionysiac Festival on the 12th day in the month Anthesterion, as
> is also the custom down to the present day with the Ionian descen-
> dants of the Athenians); and other ancient sanctuaries also are
> placed here. And the spring which is now called* Nine-Spouts,

---

[1] Thucyd. II. 15 τὸ δὲ πρὸ τούτου ἡ ἀκρόπολις ἡ νῦν οὖσα πόλις ἦν καὶ τὸ ὑπ' αὐτὴν
πρὸς νότον μάλιστα τετραμμένον· τεκμήριον δέ. τὰ γὰρ ἱερὰ ἐν αὐτῇ τῇ ἀκροπόλει καὶ
ἄλλων θεῶν ἐστί, καὶ τὰ ἔξω πρὸς τοῦτο τὸ μέρος τῆς πόλεως μᾶλλον ἵδρυται, τό τε τοῦ
Διὸς τοῦ Ὀλυμπίου καὶ τὸ Πύθιον καὶ τὸ τῆς Γῆς καὶ τὸ ἐν Λίμναις Διονύσου (ᾧ τὰ
ἀρχαιότερα Διονύσια τῇ δωδεκάτῃ ποιεῖται ἐν μηνὶ Ἀνθεστηριῶνι) ὥσπερ καὶ οἱ ἀπ'
Ἀθηναίων Ἴωνες ἔτι καὶ νῦν νομίζουσιν, ἵδρυται δὲ καὶ ἄλλα ἱερὰ ταύτῃ ἀρχαῖα. καὶ τῇ
κρήνῃ τῇ νῦν μὲν τῶν τυράννων οὕτω σκευασάντων Ἐννεακρούνῳ καλουμένῃ, τὸ δὲ πάλαι
φανερῶν τῶν πηγῶν οὐσῶν Καλλιρρόῃ ὠνομασμένῃ—ἐκείνῃ τε ἐγγὺς οὔσῃ τὰ πλείστου ἄξια
ἐχρῶντο, καὶ νῦν ἔτι ἀπὸ τοῦ ἀρχαίου πρό τε γαμικῶν καὶ ἐς ἄλλα τῶν ἱερῶν νομίζεται τῷ
ὕδατι χρῆσθαι. καλεῖται δὲ διὰ τὴν παλαιὰν ταύτῃ κατοίκησιν καὶ ἡ ἀκρόπολις μέχρι
τοῦδε ἔτι ὑπ' Ἀθηναίων πόλις.
[2] I keep the MS. reading; see Critical Note.

from the form given it by the despots, but which formerly, when the
sources were open, was named Fair-Fount—*this spring (I say),*
being near, they used for the most important purposes, and even
now it is still the custom derived from the ancient (habit) to use
the water before weddings and for other sacred purposes.   Because
of the ancient settlement here, the citadel (as well as the present
city) is still to this day called by the Athenians the City.'

In spite of certain obscurities, which are mainly due to a
characteristically Thucydidean over-condensation of style, the
main purport of the argument is clear.   Thucydides, it will be
remembered, wants to prove that the city before Theseus was,
because of its small size, incapable of holding a large town population.   This small size not being evident to the contemporaries of
Thucydides, he proceeds to define the limits of the ancient city.
He makes a statement and supports it by fourfold evidence.

The statement that he makes is that *the ancient city com-*
prised the present citadel together with what is below it towards
about south.   The fourfold evidence is as follows :

1.   The sanctuaries are in the citadel itself, those of other
deities as well as the Goddess.

2.   Those ancient sanctuaries that are outside are placed
towards this part of the present city more than elsewhere.   Four
instances of such outside shrines are adduced.

3.   There is a spring near at hand used from of old for the
most important purposes, and still so used on sacred occasions.

4.   The citadel, as well as the present city, was still in the
time of Thucydides called the 'city.'

We begin with the statement as to the limits of the city.   Not
till we clearly understand exactly what Thucydides states, how
much and how little, can we properly weigh the fourfold evidence
he offers in support of his statement.

'*Before this what is now the citadel was the city, together with*
what is below it towards about south.   The city before Theseus
was the citadel or acropolis of the days of Thucydides, *plus* something else.   The citadel or acropolis needed then, and needs now,
no further definition.   By it is clearly meant not the whole hill to
the base, but the plateau on the summit enclosed by the walls of
Themistocles and Kimon together with the fortification outworks

on the west slope still extant in the days of Thucydides. But the
second and secondary part of the statement is less clearly defined.
The words neither give nor suggest, to us at least, any circum-
scribing line; only a direction, and that vague enough, 'towards
about south.' It is a point at which the scholar naturally asks,
whether archaeology has anything to say?

But before that question is asked and answered, it should be
noted that from the shape of the sentence alone something
may be inferred. That the present citadel is coextensive with
the old city is the main contention. We feel that Thucydides
might have stopped there and yet made his point, namely, the
smallness of that ancient city. But Thucydides is a careful man,
he remembers that the two were not quite coextensive. To the old
city must be reckoned an additional portion below the citadel (τὸ
ὑπ' αὐτήν), a portion that, as will later be seen, his readers might
be peculiarly apt to forget; so he adds it to his statement. But,
by the way it is hung on, we should naturally figure that portion
as 'not only subordinate to the acropolis, but in some way closely
incorporated with it. In relation to the acropolis, this additional
area, to justify the arrangement of the words of Thucydides, should
be a part neither large nor independent[1].'

Thus much can be gathered from the text; it is time to see
what additional evidence is brought by archaeology.

Thucydides was, according to his lights, scrupulously exact.
It happens, however, that in the nature of things he could not,
as regards the limits of the ancient city, be strictly precise. The
necessary monuments were by his time hidden deep below the
ground. His first and main statement, that one portion of the
old city was coextensive with the citadel of his day, is not quite
true. This upper portion of the old burgh was a good deal
smaller; all the better for his argument, had he known it!
Thanks to systematic excavation we know more about the limits
of the old city than Thucydides himself, and it happens curiously
enough that this more exact and very recent knowledge, while
it leads us to convict Thucydides of a real and unavoidable
inexactness, gives us also the reason for his caution. It explains

---

[1] See Dr A. W. Verrall, *The Site of Primitive Athens. Thucydides* ii. 15 *and
recent explorations, Class. Rev.* June 1900, p. 274. In the discussion of the actual
text, I have throughout followed Dr Verrall.

to us why, appended to his statement about the city and the citadel, he is careful to put in the somewhat vague *addendum*, '*together with what is below it towards about south.*'

To us to-day the top of the Acropolis appears as a smooth plateau sloping gently westwards towards the Propylaea, and this plateau is surrounded by fortification walls, whose clean, straight lines show them to be artificial. Very similar in all essentials was the appearance presented by the hill to the contemporaries of Thucydides, but such was not the ancient Acropolis. What manner of thing the primitive hill was has been shown by the excavations carried on by the Greek Government from 1885–1889. The excavators, save when they were prevented by the foundations of buildings, have everywhere dug down to the living rock, every handful of the *débris* exposed has been carefully examined, and nothing more now remains for discovery.

When the traveller first reaches Athens he is so impressed by the unexpected height and dominant situation of Lycabettus, that he wonders why it plays so small a part in classical record. Plato[1] seems to have felt that it was hard for Lycabettus to be left out. In his description of primitive Athens he says, 'in old days the hill of the Acropolis extended to the Eridanus and Ilissus, and included the Pnyx on one side and Lycabettus as a boundary on the opposite side of the hill,' and there is a certain rough geological justice about Plato's description. All these hills are spurs of that last offshoot of Pentelicus, known in modern times as Turkovouni. Yet to the wise Athena, Lycabettus was but building material; she was carrying the hill through the air to fortify her Acropolis, when she met the crow[2] who told her that the disobedient sisters had opened the chest, and then and there she dropped Lycabettus and left it…to the crows.

A moment's reflection will show why the Acropolis was chosen and Lycabettus left. Lycabettus is a good hill to climb and see a sunset from. It has not level space enough for a settlement. The Acropolis has the two *desiderata* of an ancient burgh, space on which to settle, and easy defensibility.

The Acropolis, as in neolithic days the first settlers found it,

---

[1] Plat. *Kritias* 112.   [2] Antigonos, *Hist. Mirab.* 12.

was, it will be seen in Fig. 1, a long, rocky ridge, broken at intervals[1]. It could only be climbed with ease on the west and south-west sides, the remaining sides being everywhere precipitous, though in places not absolutely inaccessible. For a primitive settlement it was an ideal situation. Two things remained for the settlers to do: first, they had to level the surface

Fig. 1.

by hewing away jagged rocks and filling up cracks with earth and stones to make sites for their houses and their sanctuaries; and second, they had to supplement what nature had already done in the way of fortification; here and there to make the steep rocks steeper, build a wall round their settlement, and, above all, fortify that accessible west and south-west end and build an impregnable gateway. Kleidemos[2], writing in the fifth century B.C., says, 'they levelled the Acropolis and made the Pelasgicon, which they built round it nine-gated.' They levelled the surface, they built a wall round it, they furnished the fortification wall with gates. We begin for convenience sake with the wall. In tracing its course the process of levelling is most plainly seen. The question of the gates will be taken last.

In the plan in Fig. 2 is shown what excavations have laid bare of the ancient Pelasgic fortress. We see instantly the inexactness of the main statement of Thucydides. It is not '*what is now the Citadel*' that was the main part of the old burgh, but something substantially smaller, smaller by about one-fifth of the total area. We see also that this Thucydides could not know. The Pelasgic wall following the broken outline of the natural rock was in his days covered over by the artificial platform reaching everywhere to the wall of Kimon. At one place, and one only, in the days of

[1] W. Dörpfeld, "Ueber die Ausgrabungen auf der Akropolis," *Athen. Mitt.* XI. 1886, p. 162.

[2] ap. Suidam, s.v. Ἄπεδα el. Ἠπέδιζον: ἄπεδα, τὰ ἰσόπεδα. Κλείδημος 'καὶ ἠπέδιζον τὴν ἀκρόπολιν, περιέβαλλον δὲ ἐννεάπυλον τὸ Πελασγικόν.

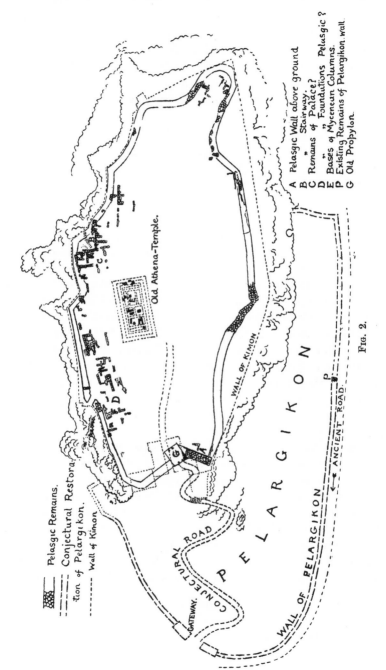

A Pelasgic Wall above ground
B   "   Stairway.
C Remains of Palace?
D   "   Foundations Pelasgic?
E Bases of Mycenean Columns.
P Existing Remains of Pelargikon wall.
G Old Propylon.

FIG. 2.

Thucydides, did the Pelasgic wall come into sight, and there it still remains above ground, as it has always been, save when temporarily covered by Turkish out-works. This visible piece is the large fragment (A), 6 metres broad, to the south of the present Propylaea and close to the earlier gateway (G). In the days of Thucydides it stood several metres high. Of this we have definite monumental evidence. The south-east corner of the wall of the south-west wing of the present Propylaea is bevelled away[1] so as to fit against this Pelasgic wall, and the bevelling can be seen to-day. This portion of the Pelasgic wall is of exceptional strength and thickness, doubtless because it was part of the gateway fortifications, the natural point of attack.

Save for this one exception, the Pelasgic walls lie now, as they did in the day of Thucydides, below the level of the present hill, and their existence was, until the excavations began, only dimly suspected. Literary tradition said there was a circuit wall, but where this circuit wall ran was matter of conjecture; bygone scholars even placed it *below* the Acropolis. Now the outline, though far from complete, is clear enough. To the south and south-west of the Parthenon there are, as seen on the plan, substantial remains and what is gone can be easily supplied. On the north side the remains are scanty. The reason is obvious; the line of the Pelasgic fortification on the south lies well within the line of Kimon's wall; the Pelasgic wall was covered in, but not intentionally broken down. To the north it coincided with Themistocles' wall, and was therefore, for the most part, pulled down or used as foundation.

But none the less is it clear that the centre of gravity of the ancient settlement lay to the north of the plateau. Although the north wall was broken away, it is on this north side that the remains which *may* belong to a royal palace have come to light. The plan of these remains cannot in detail be made out, but the general analogy of the masonry to that of Tiryns and Mycenae leave no doubt that here we have remains of 'Mycenaean' date. North-east of the Erechtheion is a rock-cut stairway (B) leading down through a natural cleft in the rock to the plain below. As at Tiryns and Mycenae, the settlement on the Acropolis had not

[1] Dörpfeld, "Die Propylaeen," *A. Mitt.* x. 1885, p. 139 and see the plan of the Propylaea in my *Myth. and Mon. Anc. Athens*, p. 352.

only its great entrance-gates, but a second smaller approach, accessible only to passengers on foot, and possibly reserved for the rulers only.

Incomplete though the remains of this settlement are, the certain fact of its existence, and its close analogy to the palaces of Tiryns and Mycenae are of priceless value. Ancient Athens is now no longer a thing by itself; it falls into line with all the other ancient 'Mycenaean' fortified hills, with Thoricus, Acharnae, Aphidna, Eleusis. The citadel of Kekrops is henceforth as the citadel of Agamemnon and as the citadel of Priam. The 'strong house' of Erechtheus is not a temple, but what the words plainly mean, the dwelling of a king. Moreover we are dealing not with a city, in the modern sense, of vague dimensions, but with a compact fortified burgh.

Thucydides, though certainly convicted of some inexactness as to detail, is in his main contention seen to be strictly true—*'what is now the citadel was the city.'* Grasping this firmly in our minds we may return to note his inexactness as to detail. By examining certain portions of the Pelasgic wall more closely, we shall realize how much smaller was the space it enclosed than the Acropolis as known to Thucydides.

The general shape of the hill, and its subsequent alteration, are best realized by Dr Dörpfeld's simple illustration[1]. A vertical section of the natural rock, it is roughly of the shape of a house (Fig. 3) with an ordinary gable roof. The sides of the house represent the steep inaccessible cliffs to north and south and east; the lines of the roof slope like the lines of the upper part of the hill converging at the middle. Suppose the sides of the house produced upwards to the height of the roof-ridge, and the triangular space so formed filled in, we have the state of the Acropolis when Kimon's walls were completed. The filling in of those

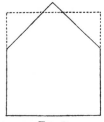

FIG. 3.

spaces is the history of the gradual 'levelling of the surface of the hill, the work of many successive generations.' The section in Fig. 4 will show that this levelling up had to be done chiefly

---

[1] Dörpfeld, 'Ausgrabungen auf der Akropolis,' *A. Mitt.* XI. 1896, p. 167.

on the north and south sides; to the east and west the living
rock is near the surface.

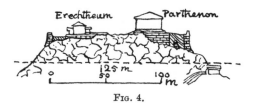

FIG. 4.

It has already been noted that on the north side of the
Acropolis the actual remains of the Pelasgian wall are few and
slight; but as the wall of Themistocles which superseded it
follows the contours of the rock, we may be sure that here the
two were nearly coincident.   The wall of Themistocles remains
to this day a perpetual monument of the disaster wrought by the
Persians.   Built into it opposite the Erechtheum, not by accident,
but for express memorial, are fragments of the architrave, triglyphs
and cornice of poros stone, and the marble metopes, from the old
temple of Athena which the Persians had burnt.   Other memorials
lay buried out of sight, and were brought to light by the excavations of 1886.   The excavators[1] were clearing the ground to the
north-east of the Propylaea.   On the 6th of February, at a depth
of from 3—4½ metres below the surface, they came upon fourteen
of the 'Maidens[2].'   The section[3] in Fig. 5 shows the place where
they had slept their long sleep.   We should like to think they
were laid there in all reverence for their beauty, but hard facts
compel us to own that, though their burial may have been
prompted in part by awe of their sanctity, yet the practical
Athenian did not shrink from utilizing them as material to level
up with.

The deposit, it is here clearly seen, was in three strata.   Each
stratum consisted of statues and fragments of statues, inscribed
bases, potsherds, charred wood, stones, and earth.   Each stratum,
and this is the significant fact, is separated from the one above it
by a thin layer of rubble, the refuse of material used in the wall

[1] Dr Kabbadias, *Fouilles de l'Acropole*, 1886, Pl. I. and descriptive text.
[2] The discussion and interpretation of these figures is reserved for p. 51.
[3] Ἐφήμερις Ἀρχαιολογική, 1866, p. 78.

of Themistocles.   The conclusion to the architect is manifest.
In building the wall, perhaps to save expense, no scaffolding was
used; but, after a few courses were laid, the ground inside

Fig. 5.

was levelled up, and for this purpose what could be better than
the statues knocked down by the Persians?   Headless, armless,
their sanctity was gone, their beauty uncared for.   In the topmost of the three strata—the stratum which yielded the first
find of 'Maidens'—a hoard of coins was found: thirty-five Attic
tetradrachms, two drachmas, and twenty-three obols.   All are of
Solon's time except eight of the obols, which date somewhat
earlier.   Besides the 'Maidens,' on this north side of the Acropolis
other monuments came to light, many bronzes, and among them
the lovely flat Athena[1], the beautiful terra-cotta plaque[2] painted
with the figure of a hoplite, and countless votive terra-cottas.

The excavations on the south side of the Acropolis have
yielded much that is of great value for art and for science, for
our knowledge of the extent of the Pelasgian fortification, results
of the first importance.   The section in Fig. 7, taken at the

[1] *Eph. Arch.* 1887, pl. 4.   [2] *Eph. Arch.* 1887, pl. 8.

south-east corner of the Parthenon, shows the state of things
revealed. The section should be compared with the view in
Fig. 6.

The masonry marked 2 is the foundation, deep and massive
beyond all expectation, laid, not for the Parthenon as we know it,

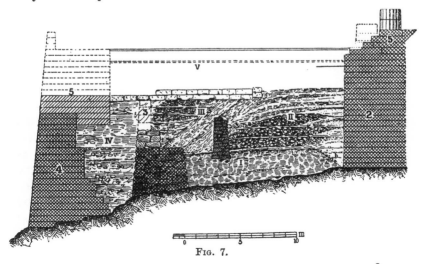

Fig. 7.

but for that earlier Parthenon begun before the Persian War, and fated never to be completed. At 4 we see the great Kimonian wall as it exists to-day, though obscured by its mediaeval casing. All this, if we want to realize primitive Athens, we must think away. The date of Kimon's wall is of course roughly fixed as shortly after 469 B.C., the foundations of the early Parthenon are certainly before the Persian War, probably after the date of Peisistratos. We may probably, though not quite certainly, attribute them to the time of the first democracy, the activity of Kleisthenes[1], a period that saw the building of the theatre-shaped Pnyx, the establishment of the new agora in the Kerameikos, and the Stoa of the Athenians at Delphi. Laurium had just begun to yield silver from her mines. Themistocles, before and after the war, was all for fortification; the Alkmaeonid Kleisthenes may well have indulged an hereditary tendency to temple building.

Save for the clearing of our minds, the date of the early temple-foundations does not immediately concern us. Their importance is that, but for the building of the Parthenon, early and late, we should never apparently have had the great alteration and addition to the south side of the hill and the ancient Pelasgian wall would never have been covered in. Let us see how this happened[2].

We start with nothing but the natural rock, and on it the Pelasgian wall (1). Over the natural rock is a layer of earth, marked I. Whatever objects have been found in that layer date before the laying of the great foundations; these objects are chiefly fragments of pottery, many of them of 'Mycenean' character, and some ordinary black-figured vases.

It is decided to build a great temple, and the foundations are to be laid. The ground slopes away somewhat rapidly, so the southern side of the temple is to be founded on an artificial platform. The trench (*b*) is dug in the layer of earth; then, just as on the north side of the hill, no scaffolding is used, but as the foundations are laid course by course, the *débris* is used as a platform for the workmen. A supporting wall (2) is required and built of polygonal masonry; it rises course by course, corresponding

---

[1] Dörpfeld, 'Die Zeit des älteren Parthenon,' *A. Mitt.* 1902, p. 410.
[2] *A. Mitt.* 1892, p. 158, pl. VIII. and IX.

with the platform of *débris*. And then, what might have been expected but was apparently not foreseen, happens. The slender wall can be raised no higher and at about the second course the *débris* unsupported pours over it, as seen at III.

The *débris*, unchecked, fell over as far as the old Pelasgian wall. How high this originally stood it is not possible now to say; but, from the fact that outside the supporting wall the layers of *débris* again lie horizontally, and from the analogy of another section taken further west, which need not be discussed here, it is probable that the old wall was raised by several new courses, and that the higher ones were of quadrangular blocks, as restored in Fig. 7.

So far all that has been accomplished is the raising of the old Pelasgian wall and a levelling up of the terrace to its new height. That these terraces were raised step by step with the foundations of the Parthenon is clear. Between each layer of earth and poros fragments—just as we have seen in the similar circumstances of the north wall (p. 15)—is interposed a layer of splinters and fragments of the stones used in the building of the foundations. This can clearly be seen at II. in the section in Fig. 7.

It may seem strange that Kleisthenes, or whoever built the earlier Parthenon, did not at once utilize the Pelasgian wall and boldly pile up his terrace against its support. But it must be remembered that the space between the Parthenon and the Pelasgian wall was very great; an immense amount of *débris* would be required for the filling up of such a space, and it was probably more economical to build the polygonal supporting-wall nearer to the Parthenon. Anyhow it is quite clear that the polygonal wall was no provisional structure. Its façade shows it was meant to be seen, and that the terrace was meant for permanent use is clear from the fact that it is connected by a flight of steps with the lower terrace under the Pelasgian wall (Fig. 8). It is clear that whoever planned these steps never thought that the lower terrace would be levelled up.

Doubtless whoever filled in the terrace to the height of the raised Pelasgian wall believed in like manner that his work was complete. But Kimon thought otherwise. We know for certain that it was he who built the great final wall, the structure that remains to-day, though partly concealed by mediaeval casing Fig. 7 (4).

2—2

Plutarch[1] tells us that after the battle of Eurymedon (469 B.C.) so much money was raised by the sale of the spoils of the Persians

FIG. 8.

that the people were able to afford to build the south wall.   We know also that this wall of Kimon was at least as much a retaining wall to the great terrace as a fortification.   For the filling up of the space between the Pelasgian fortification and his own wall Kimon had material sadly ample.   He had the *débris* left by the Persians after the sacking of the Acropolis.   The fragments of sculpture and architecture that bear traces of fire are found in the strata marked IV, and there only, for it is these strata only that were laid down after the Persian War[2].   The last courses of 'Kimon's wall' (5) were laid by Perikles, and he it was who finally filled in the terrace to its present level (V).

The relation of the successive walls and terraces is shown by

---

[1] Plut. *Vit. Cim.* 13.

[2] Unfortunately at the actual time of the excavations the chronology of the various retaining walls was not clearly evident and the precise place where many of the fragments excavated were found was not noted with adequate precision.

the ground-plan in Fig. 9[1]. The double shaded lines from A to
E and D show the irregular course of the old Pelasgic wall. The

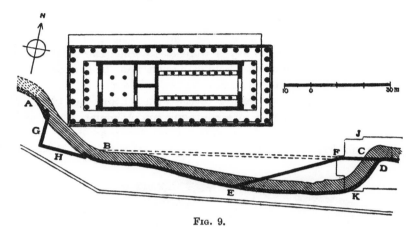

FIG. 9.

dotted lines from B to F show the polygonal supporting wall of
the first terrace.   It ran, as is seen, nearly parallel to the
Parthenon. Its course is lost to sight after it passes under the
new museum, but originally it certainly joined the Pelasgic wall
at C. At B was the stairway joining the two terraces. Next
came the time when, as the rubble fell over the wall, larger space
was needed, and a portion of the Pelasgic wall was utilized and
raised.   This is shown by the thick black line from B to E coincident with the Pelasgic wall; the masonry here was of quadrangular
poros blocks. The coincidence with the Pelasgic wall was only
partial. At GH there jutted out an independent angular outpost,
and again at EF the new wall is separate from the old ; at FD it
coincided with the earlier polygonal terrace wall. Kimon's wall
is indicated by the outside double lines, and in the space between
these lines and the wall HEK lay the *débris* of the Persian War.
Above that *débris* lay a still later stratum, deposited during the
building operations of Perikles.

The various terraces and walls have been examined somewhat
in detail, because their examination helps us to realize as nothing
else could how artificial a structure is the south side of the Acro-

[1] *A. Mitt.* xxvii. 1902, p. 398, Fig. 5.

polis, and also—a point, to us, of paramount importance—how different was the early condition of the hill from its later appearance.

Before we pass to the consideration of the second clause in the historian's statement, '*together with what is below it towards about south*,' it is necessary to say a word as to when the old fortress walls were built and by whom.   Kimon and Themistocles we know, but who were these earlier master-builders ?

A red-figured vase painter of the fifth century B.C. gives us what would have seemed to a contemporary Athenian a safe and satisfactory answer—'There were giants in those days.'   The design in Fig. 10 is from a skyphos[1] in the Louvre Museum.

FIG. 10.

Athena is about to fortify her chosen hill.   She wears no aegis, for her work is peaceful ; she has planted her spear in the ground perhaps as a measuring rod, and she has chosen her workman. A great giant, his name *Gigas*, inscribed over him, toils after her, bearing a huge 'Cyclopean' rock.   She points with her hand where he is to lay it.

On the obverse of the same vase (Fig. 11) we have a scene of similar significance.   To either side of a small tree, which marks the background as woodland, stands a man of rather wild and

[1] F. Hauser, *Strena Helbigiana*, p. 115.   The reverse was first correctly explained thro' the identification of the σταφύλη by Dr O. Rossbach, 'Verschollene Sagen und Kulten,' *Neue Jahrbücher f. Kl. Altertumswissenschaft*, 1901, p. 390.

uncouth appearance. The man to the left is bearded and his
name is inscribed, *Phlegyas*. The right-hand man is younger,
and obviously resembles the giant of the obverse. He is showing
to Phlegyas an object, which they both inspect with an intent,

Fig. 11.

puzzled air. And well they may. It is a builder's *staphyle*[1], or
measuring line, weighted with knobs of lead like a cluster of
grapes; hence its name. Phlegyas[2] and his giant Thessalian folk
were the typical lawless bandits of antiquity; they plundered
Delphi, they attacked Thebes after it had been fortified by
Amphion and Zethus. But Athena has them at her hest for
master-builders. All glory to Athena!

It is not only at Athens that legends of giant, fabulous workmen cluster about 'Mycenean' remains. Phlegyas and his giants
toil for Athena, and at Tiryns too, according to tradition, the
Kyklopes work for King Proetus[3], and they too built the walls
and Lion-Gate of Mycenae[4]. At Thebes the Kadmeia[5] is the
work of Amphion and Zethus, sons of the gods, and the fashion
in which art represents Zethus as toiling is just that of our
giant on the vase. The mantle that Jason wore was embroidered
Apollonius of Rhodes[6] tells us, with the building of Thebes,

[1] *Il.* ii. 765...ἵπποι σταφύλῃ ἐπὶ νῶτον ἐΐσαι.
[2] See Roscher, *Lex.* s.v.
[3] Paus. ii. 25. 7.   [4] Paus. ii. 16. 5.
[5] Paus. ix. 5. 6.   [6] Apoll. Rhod. i. 736.

> Of river-born Antiope therein
> The sons were woven, Zethus and his twin
> Amphion, and all Thebes unlifted yet
> Around them lay. They sought but now to set
> The stones of her first building. Like one sore
> In labour, Zethus on great shoulders bore
> A stone-clad mountain's crest; and there hard by
> Amphion went his way with minstrelsy
> Clanging a golden lyre, and twice as vast
> The dumb rock rose and sought him as he passed.

Sisyphos, ancient king of Corinth, built on the acropolis of Corinth his great palace, the Sisypheion. He is the Corinthian double of Erechtheus with his Erechtheion. Strabo[1] was in doubt whether to call the Sisypheion palace or temple. Like the old Erechtheion, it was both fortress and sanctuary. In Hades for eternal remembrance, not, as men later thought, of his sin, but of his craft as master-builder, Sisyphos[2], like Zethus, like our giant, still rolls a huge stone up the slope. Everywhere it is the same tale. All definite record or remembrance of the building of 'Cyclopean' walls is lost; some hero-king built them, some god, some demi-god, some giant. Just so did the devil in ancient days build his Bridges all over England.

Tradition loves to embroider a story with names and definite details. The prudent Attic vase-painter gives us only a nameless 'Giant.' Others knew more. Pausanias[3] had heard the builders' actual names and tried to fix their race. He tells us—just as he leaves the Acropolis—'Save for the portion built by Kimon, son of Miltiades, the whole circuit of the Acropolis fortification was, they say, built by the Pelasgians, who once dwelt below the Acropolis. It is said that Agrolas and Hyperbios...and on asking who they were, I could only learn that in origin they were Sikelians and that they migrated to Acarnania.'

Spite of the lacuna, it is clear that Agrolas and Hyperbios are the reputed builders. The reference to Sicily dates probably from a time when the Kyklopes had taken up their abode in the island. The two builder-brothers remind us of Amphion and Zethus, and of their prototypes the Dioscuri[4]. Pliny[5] tells of a similar pair,

[1] Strabo, VIII. 21 § 379. See my *Prolegomena*, p. 609.
[2] *Od.* XI. 594. Mr Salomon Reinach in his "Sisyphe aux enfers et quelques autres damnés,' *Rev. Arch.* 1903, has established beyond doubt the true interpretation of the stone of Sisyphos.
[3] Paus. I. 28. 3.   [4] Dr Rendel Harris, *The Dioscuri*, p. 8.
[5] Plin. *Nat. Hist.* VII. 57.

though he gives to one of them another name. ʻThe brothers Euryalos and Hyperbios were the first to make brick-kilns and houses at Athens; before this they used caves in the ground for houses.'

The names of the two ʻPelasgian' brothers are, as we know from the evidence of vase-paintings[1], ʻgiant' names, and *Hyperbios* is obviously appropriate. The names leave us in the region of myth, but the tradition that the brothers were ʻPelasgian' deserves closer attention.

In describing the old wall we have spoken of it as ʻ Pelasgian,' and in this we follow classical tradition. Quoting from Hecataeus (circ. 500 B.C.), Herodotus[2] speaks of land under Hymettus as given to the Pelasgians ʻin payment for the fortification wall which they had formerly built round the Acropolis.' Again, Herodotus[3] tells how when Kleomenes King of Sparta reached Athens, he, together with those of the citizens who desired to be free, besieged the despots who were shut up in the Pelasgian fortification.'

A Pelasgian fortification, a constant tradition that Athens was inhabited by Pelasgians—we seem to be on solid ground. Yet on a closer examination the evidence for connecting the name of the fortification with the name ʻ Pelasgian' crumbles. In the one official[4] inscription that we possess the word is written, not Pelasgikon, but Pelargikon. In like manner, in Thucydides[5], where the word occurs twice, it is written with an *r*. Pelargikon is ʻstork-fort,' not Pelasgian fort. The confusion probably began with Herodotus, who was specially interested in the Pelasgians.

Why the old citadel was called ʻ stork-fort' we cannot say— there are no storks there now—but we have one delightful piece of evidence that, to the Athenian of the sixth century B.C., ʻ*stork-fort*' was a reality. Immediately to the south of the present Erechtheion lie the foundations of the ancient Doric temple[6], currently known by a

---

[1] For *Euryalos* see *Eph. Arch.* 1885, Taf. v. 2 and 3. For *Hyperbios, Mon. d. Inst.* vi. and vii.

[2] Herod. vi. 137 μισθὸν τοῦ τείχεος τοῦ περὶ τὴν ἀκρόπολίν ποτε ἐληλαμένου.

[3] Herod. v. 64 ἐπολιόρκεε τοὺς τυράννους ἀπεργμένους ἐν τῷ Πελασγικῷ τείχει. All the mss. except Z have Πελασγικῷ: Z has been corrected to Πελαργικῷ.

[4] *C.I.A.* iv. 2. 27. 6...ἐν τῷ Πελαργικῷ...ἐκ τοῦ Πελαργικοῦ.

[5] In the best ms. (Laur. C).

[6] For details of this temple, see my *Myth. and Mon. Anc. Athens*, p. 496. For its ground-plan, see below p. 40, Fig. 18.

pardonable Germanism as the 'old Athena-temple.' For its date
we have a certain *terminus ante quem*. The colonnade was of the
time of Peisistratos; it was a later addition; the cella of the
temple existed before—how much before we do not know. The
zeal and skill of Prof. Dörpfeld for architecture, of Drs Wiegand
and Schrader for sculpture, have restored to us a picture of that
ancient Doric temple all aglow with life and colour and in essentials complete[1].

Of all the marvellous fragments of early sculpture recently discovered, none is more widely known
nor more justly popular than the smiling, three-headed monster known
throughout Europe as the 'Blue-
beard.' He belongs to the
sculptures of the west pediment of the inner pre-
Peisistratean cella of the
'old Athena-temple,'
a portion of which

Fig. 12.

is shown in Fig. 12. It is tempting to turn aside and discuss
in detail the whole pediment composition to which he belongs.
It will, however, shortly be seen (p. 37) that our argument

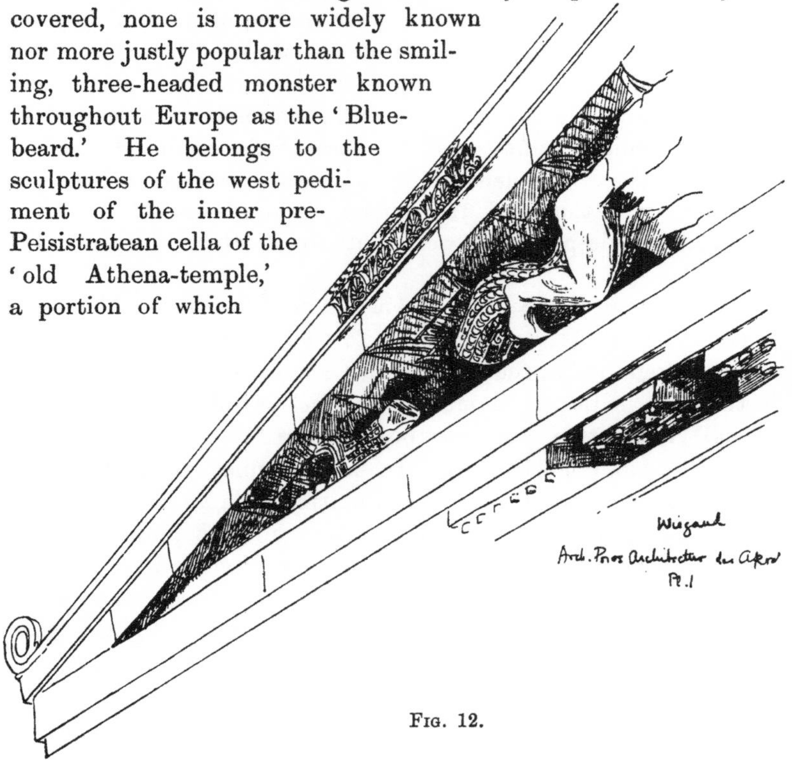

---

[1] Wiegand-Schrader-Dörpfeld, *Poros-Architektur der Akropolis*. For any realization of pre-Periclean architecture a study of the coloured plates of this work is
essential.

forbids all detailed discussion of the sanctuaries of Athena, and the pediments of her earliest temple have therefore, for us at the moment, an interest merely incidental.

Thus much, however, for clearness sake may and must be said. The design of the western pediment fell into two parts. In one angle, that to the left of the spectator, Herakles is wrestling with Triton; the right-hand portion, not figured here, is occupied by the triple figure of 'Blue-beard,' whose correct mythological name is probably Typhon[1]. He is no protagonist, only a splendid smiling spectator. The centre of the pediment, where, in the art of Pheidias, we should expect the interest to culminate, was occupied by accessories, the stem of a tree on which hung, as in vase-paintings, the bow and arrows and superfluous raiment of Herakles.

It is a point of no small mythological interest that in this and two other primitive pediments the protagonist is not, as we should expect, the indigenous hero Theseus, but the semi-Oriental Herakles; but this question also we must set aside; our immediate interest is not in the sculptured figures of the pediment, but in the richly painted decoration on the pediment roof above their heads.

The recent excavations on the Acropolis yielded a large number of painted architectural fragments, the place and significance of which was at first far from clear. Of these fragments forty were adorned with two forms of lotus-flower; twenty had upon them figures of birds of two sorts. Fragmentary though the birds mostly are, the two kinds (storks and sea-eagles) are, by realism as to feathers, beak, legs, and claws, carefully distinguished. The stork (πελαργός) in the Pelargikon is a surprise and a delight. Was Aristophanes[2] thinking of this Pelargikon when to the building of his Nephelokokkygia he brought

For brickmakers a myriad flight of storks.

[1] Typhon and Tritons appear together on the throne of Apollo at Amyclae. The artistic motives of this Ionian work are largely Oriental. The conjunction of Typhon and the Tritons is not, I think, a mere decorative chance. Attention has not, I think, been called, in connection with this pediment, to the fact that in Plutarch's *Isis and Osiris* (xxxii.) Typhon *is* the sea into which the Nile flows (Τυφῶνα δὲ τὴν θάλασσαν, εἰς ἣν ὁ Νεῖλος ἐμπίπτων ἀφανίζεται). The Egyptian inspiration of the *Isis and Osiris* no one will deny, and on this Egyptianized pediment with its lotus-flowers the Egyptian sea-god Typhon is well in place. His name is doubtless, as Muss Arnolt *Semitic Words in Greek and Latin*, p. 59 points out, connected with Heb. צָפוֹן hidden, dark, northern. The sea was north of Egypt.

[2] Ar. *Av.* 1139   ἕτεροι δ᾽ ἐπλινθοποίουν πελαργοὶ μύριοι.

One of the storks is given in Fig. 13. The birds in the original
fragments are brilliantly and delicately coloured.   Their vivid red

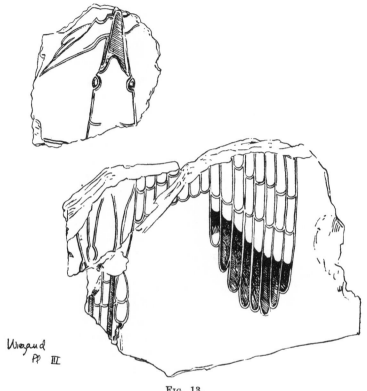

Fɪɢ. 13.

legs take us to Delphi. We remember Ion[1] with his laurel crown,
his bow and arrows, his warning song to swan and eagle.

> There see! the birds are up: they fly
> Their nests upon Parnassus high
> And hither tend.   I warn you all
> To golden house and marble wall
> Approach not.   Once again my bow
> Zeus' herald-bird, will lay thee low;
> Of all that fly the mightiest thou
> In talon! Lo another now
> Sails hitherward—a swan! Away
> Away, thou red-foot!

[1] Eur. *Ion* 154, trans. by Dr Verrall.

In days when on open-air altars sacrifice smoked, and there was abundance of sacred cakes, birds were real and very frequent presences. To the heads of numbers of statues found on the Acropolis is fixed a sharp spike to prevent the birds perching[1]. They were sacred yet profane.

The lotus-flowers carry us back to Egypt. The rich blending of motives from the animal and vegetable kingdom is altogether 'Mycenaean.' Man in art, as in life, is still at home with his brothers the fish, the bird, and the flower. After this ancient fulness and warmth of life a pediment by Pheidias strikes a chill. Its sheer humanity is cold and lonely. Man has forgotten that

> Earth is a covering to hide thee, the garment of thee.

There are two sorts of birds, two sorts of lotus-flowers, and there are two pediments. It is natural to suppose, with Dr Wiegand, that the eagles belonged to the east, the principal pediment. There, it will later be seen (p. 47), were seated the divinities of the place. Our pediment decorated the west end, the humbler seat of heroes rather than gods. There Herakles wrestled with the Triton; there old Blue-beard—surely a monster of the earlier slime—kept his watch; and over that ancient struggle of hero and monster brooded the stork.

The storks themselves are there to remind us that the old name of the citadel was Pelargikon, and that Pelargikon meant 'stork fort'; by an easy shift it became Pelasgikon[2], and had henceforth an etymologically false association with the Pelasgoi. Etymologically false, but perhaps in fact true, for happily the analogy between the Pelargic walls and those of Mycenae is beyond dispute, and if the 'Mycenaeans' were Pelasgian, the walls are, after all, Pelasgic.

We have seen that both Thucydides and the official inscription write Pelargikon; their statements will repay examination.

Thucydides, after his account of the narrow limits of the city before Theseus, returns to the main burden of his narrative, the crowding of the inhabitants of Attica within the city walls.

[1] See Lechat, *Au Musée de l'Acropole d'Athènes*, p. 215.
[2] Any learned blunderer might write Πελασγικόν for Πελαργικόν, but if Πελασγικόν were the original form it would be little likely to be changed to Πελαργικόν.

'Some few,' he says[1], 'indeed had dwelling places, and took refuge with some of their friends or relations, but the most part of them took up their abode on the waste places of the city and in the sanctuaries and hero-shrines, with the exception of the Acropolis and the Eleusinion, and any other that might be definitely closed. And what is called the Pelargikon beneath the Acropolis, to dwell in which was accursed, and was forbidden in the fag end of an actual Pythian oracle on this wise,

The Pelargikon better unused,

was, notwithstanding, in consequence of the immediate pressure thickly populated.'

The passage comes for a moment as something of a shock. We have been thinking of the Pelargikon as the Acropolis, we have traced its circuit of walls *on* the Acropolis, and now suddenly we find the two sharply distinguished. The Acropolis, though closed, is surely not cursed. The Acropolis is one of the definitely closed places, to which the refugees cannot get access; the Pelargikon, though accursed, is open to them, and they take possession of it; the two manifestly cannot be coincident. But happily the words 'below the Acropolis' bring recollection, and with it illumination. What is called the Pelargikon *below the Acropolis* is surely that appanage of the citadel which Thucydides in his second clause mentions so vaguely. The ancient *polis* comprised not only '*what is now the citadel*,' but also together with it, '*what is below it towards about south*[2].' Thucydides would have saved a world of trouble if he had stated that 'what is below towards the south' *was* the Pelargikon; but he does not, probably because he is concerned with dimensions, not with nomenclature.

The Pelasgikon meant originally the whole citadel, the ancient city as defined by Thucydides. This was its meaning in the days of Herodotus. In the Pelasgikon the tyrants were besieged (p. 25). But by the time of Thucydides the Acropolis proper, i.e. much the

---

[1] Thucyd. II. 17 τό τε Πελαργικὸν καλούμενον τὸ ὑπὸ τὴν ἀκρόπολιν, ὃ καὶ ἐπάρατόν τε ἦν μὴ οἰκεῖν καί τι καὶ Πυθικοῦ μαντείου ἀκροτελεύτιον τοιόνδε διεκώλυε, λέγον ὡς τὸ Πελαργικὸν ἀργὸν ἄμεινον, ὅμως ὑπὸ τῆς παραχρῆμα ἀνάγκης ἐξῳκήθη. Thucydides calls 'τὸ Πελαργικὸν ἀργὸν ἄμεινον' a final hemistich. Mr A. B. Cook kindly points out to me that it is in fact a complete line of the ancient metrical form preceding the hexameter and known as *paroimiac.*

[2] καὶ τὸ ὑπ' αὐτὴν μάλιστα πρὸς νότον τετραμμένον.

larger and more important part of the old city, had ceased to be 'Pelasgic'; the old fortifications were concealed by the new retaining walls of Themistocles and Kimon. It was only at the west and south-west that the Pelasgic fortifications were still visible, hence this portion below the Acropolis took to itself the name that had belonged to the whole; but this limited use of the word was at first tentative. Thucydides says, 'which is *called* the Pelargikon.' This is quite different from the definite 'the Pelasgian citadel' used by Herodotus. The neuter adjectival form is, so far as I know, never used of the whole complex of the Acropolis *plus* what is below.

From Thucydides we learn only that what was called the Pelargikon was *below* the Acropolis. 'Below' means immediately, vertically below, for when, in Lucian's *Fisherman*[1], Parrhesiades, after baiting his hook with figs and gold, casts down his line to fish for the false philosophers, Philosophy, seeing him hanging over, asks, 'What are you fishing for, Parrhesiades? Stones from the Pelasgikon?' An inscription[2] of the latter end of the fifth century confirms the curse mentioned by Thucydides, and shows us that the Pelargikon was a well-defined area, as it was the subject of special legislation. 'The king (i.e. the magistrate of that name) is to fix the boundaries of the sanctuaries in the Pelargikon, and henceforth altars are not to be set up in the Pelargikon without the consent of the Council and the people, nor may stones be quarried from the Pelargikon, nor earth or stones had out of it. And if any man break these enactments he shall pay 500 drachmas and the king shall report him to the Council.' Pollux[3] further tells us that there was a penalty of 3 drachmas and costs for even mowing grass within the Pelargikon, and three officers called paredroi guarded against the offence. Evidently the fortifications of the Pelargikon, partially dismantled by the Persians, had become a popular stone quarry; as evidently the state had no intention that these fortifications should fall into complete disuse. The question naturally arises, what was the purport of this surviving Pelargikon, why did it not perish with the rest of the Pelasgic fortifications?

The answer is simple: the Pelargikon remained because it was

---

[1] Lucian, *Piscator*, 46.   [2] *C.I.A.* IV. 2. 27. 6.
[3] Poll. *On.* VIII. 101.

the great fortification of the citadel gates.   According to Kleidemos, it will be remembered (p. 11), the work of the early settlers was threefold; they levelled the surface of the citadel, they built a wall round it, and they furnished the fortifications with gates. Where will those gates be ?   A glance at the section in Fig. 1 shows that they *must be* where they *are*, i.e. at the only point where the rock has an approachable slope, the west or south-west. We say advisedly *south*-west.   The great gate of Mnesicles, the Propylaea which remain to-day, face due west; but within that great gate still remain the foundations[1] of a smaller, older gate (Fig. 2, G), built in direct connection with the great Pelasgic fortification wall, and that older gate, there before the Persian War[2], faces *south*-west.

This gate facing south-west stands on the summit of the hill, and is but one.   Kleidemos (p. 11) tells us that the Pelargikon had nine gates.   That there should be nine gates *round* the Acropolis is unthinkable, such an arrangement would weaken the fortification, not strengthen it.   The successive gates must

Omont &
Carrey
Athènes en XVII᷍ siècle
.Plate XXXVII.

FIG. 14.

somehow have been arranged one inside the other, and the fortifications would probably be in terrace form.   The west slope of the Acropolis lends itself to such an arrangement, and in Turkish days this slope was occupied by a succession of redoubts (Fig. 14).

[1] Dörpfeld, 'Die Propyläen 1 und 2,' *A. Mitt.* x. 1885, pp. 38 and 131 and see my *Mon. and Myth. Ancient Athens*, p. 353.
[2] Dörpfeld, *A. Mitt.* xxvii. 1902, p. 405.

Fortified Turkish Athens is in some ways nearer to the old Pelasgian fortress than the Acropolis as we see it to-day. We shall probably not be far wrong if we think of the approach to the ancient citadel as a winding way (Fig. 15), leading gradually up by successive terraces, passing through successive fortified gates[1], and reaching at last the topmost *propylon* which faced south-west. These terraces, gates, fortifications, covering a large space, the limits of which will presently be defined,

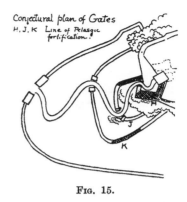

FIG. 15.

formed a whole known from the time of Thucydides to that of Lucian as the Pelargikon or Pelasgikon.

Lucian indeed not only affords our best evidence that, down to Roman days, a place called the Pelasgikon existed below the Acropolis, but is also our chief literary source for defining its limits. We expect those limits to be wide, otherwise the refugees would not have crowded in.

The passages about the Pelasgikon in Lucian are two. First in the 'Double Indictment[2],' Dike, standing on the Acropolis, sees Pan approaching, and asks who the god is with the horns and the pipe and the hairy legs. Hermes answers that Pan, who used to dwell on Mt Parthenion, had for his services been honoured with a cave below the Acropolis 'a little beyond the Pelasgikon.' There he lives and pays his taxes as a resident alien. The site of Pan's cave is certainly known; close below it was the Pelasgikon. This marks the extreme limit of the Pelasgikon to the north, for the sanctuary of Aglauros (p. 81) by which the Persians climbed up was unquestionably outside the fortifications. Herodotus[3] dis-

---

[1] The number of these gates is of course purely conjectural. The sketch in Fig. 15 which I owe to the kindness of Prof. Dörpfeld gives five only on the western slope. The line of the walls HJK is suggested by remains of the 6th century B.C. which probably occupy the site of still earlier Pelasgic fortifications (see p. 35 note 2). Of the remaining gates one would probably be near where the Asklepieion was later built and one or more on the north slope.

[2] Lucian, *Bis Accus.* 9 μικρὸν ὑπὲρ τοῦ Πελασγικοῦ.

[3] Herod. VIII. 52.

H. 3

tinctly says, 'In front then of the Acropolis, but behind the
gates and the ascent, where neither did anyone keep guard, nor
could it be expected that anyone could climb up there, some of
them ascended near the sanctuary of Aglauros, daughter of
Kekrops, though the place was precipitous.'

A second passage[1] in Lucian gives us a further clue.
Parrhesiades and Philosophy, from their station on the Acropolis,
are watching the philosophers as they crowd up. Parrhesiades
says, 'Goodness, why, at the mere sound of the words, "a ten-
pound note," the whole way up is a mass of them shouldering
each other; some are coming along the Pelasgikon, others and
more of them by the Areopagos, some are at the tomb of Talos,
and others have got ladders and put them against the Anakeion;
and, by Jove, there's a whole hive of them swarming up like bees.'
A description like this cannot be regarded as definite proof; but,
taking the shrines in their natural order, it certainly looks as
though in Lucian's days the Pelasgikon extended from the Areopagos to the Asklepieion. The philosophers crowd up by the
regular approach (ἄνοδος) to the Propylaea; there is not room for
them all, so they spread to right and left, on the right to the
Asklepieion, on the left to the Areopagos; some are crowded out
still further on the right to the tomb of Talos[2], near the
theatre of Dionysos; on the left to the Anakeion[3] on the north
side of the Acropolis.

Yet one more topographical hint is left us. In a fragment of
Polemon[4] (circ. 180 B.C.), preserved to us by the scholiast on the
Oedipus Coloneus of Sophocles, we hear that Hesychos, the
eponymous hero of the Hesychidae, hereditary priests of the
Semnae, had a sanctuary. Its position is thus described: 'it is
alongside of the Kyloneion outside the Nine-Gates.' It is clear that
in the days of Polemon either the Nine-Gates were still standing,
or their position was exactly known. It is also clear that, whatever
was called the Nine-Gates was near the precinct of the Semnae.
The eponymous hero of their priests must have had his shrine in

---

[1] Lucian, *Piscator* 42.
[2] See *Mon. and Myth. Ancient Athens*, p. 299.   [3] *Op. cit.* p. 152.
[4] Polem. ap. Schol. *Oed. Col.* 489 καθάπερ Πολέμων ἐν τοῖς πρὸς Ἐρατοσθένην
φησίν, οὕτω...κριὸν Ἡσύχῳ ἱερὸν ἥρω...οὗ τὸ ἱερόν ἐστι παρὰ τὸ Κυλώνειον, ἐκτὸς τῶν
ἐννέα πυλῶν. The MS. has Κυδώνιον, the emendation, which seems certain, is due to
C. O. Mueller.

or close to the sanctuary of the goddesses. Moreover the Kyloneion or hero shrine ties us to the same spot. When the fellow-conspirators of Kylon were driven from the Acropolis, where Megacles dared not kill them, they fastened themselves by a thread to the image of the goddess to keep themselves in touch; when they reached the altars of the Semnae the thread broke and they were all murdered[1]. The Kyloneion must have been erected as an expiatory shrine on the spot.

When we turn to examine actual remains of the Pelasgikon on the south slope of the Acropolis (Fig. 2), we are met by disappointment. Of all the various terraces and supporting walls, only one fragment (P) can definitely be pronounced Pelasgian. The remaining walls seen in Fig. 16 date between the seventh and the fifth centuries. The walls marked G in the plan in Fig. 16, but purposely omitted in Fig. 2, are of good polygonal masonry, and must have been supporting walls to the successive terraces of the Pelasgikon; they are probably of the time of Peisistratos[2], but may even be earlier. It is important to note that though not 'Pelasgic' themselves they doubtless supplanted previous 'Pelasgic' structures. The line followed by the ancient road must have skirted the outermost wall of the Pelargikon; later it was diverted in order to allow of the building of the Odeion of Herodes Atticus. The Pelasgikon of Lucian's day only extended as far as the Asklepieion; the earlier fortification must have included what was later the Asklepieion[3], as it would need to protect the important well within that precinct.

Thucydides has stated the limits of the ancient city, '*what is now the citadel was the city together with what is below it towards about south.*' We nowadays should not question his statement.

---

[1] Plut. *Vit. Solon.* xii. and Thucyd. i. 126.

[2] For these details about the date of the various walls I am indebted to Professor Dörpfeld. Dr F. Noack holds that the nine-gated Pelargikon was not of Mycenaean date but was built by Peisistratos, the earlier Pelargikon being a much simpler structure. Prof. Dörpfeld also holds that there was no nine-gated Pelargikon in Mycenaean days, but he believes that the Peisistratids only strengthened an already existing fortification, building perhaps some additional gates. The Enneapylon would then have its contemporary analogy in the Enneakrounos. See F. Noack, *Arne, A. Mitt.* 1898, p. 418.

[3] A protest was raised against the building of the Asklepieion after it was begun; possibly this was because of its encroachment on the Pelargikon. See A. Koerte, *A. Mitt.* 1896, pp. 318—331.

The remains of the Pelasgian fortifications disclosed by excavation amply support his main contention, namely, that *what is now the citadel was the city*, the conformation of the hill and literary evidence justify his careful 'addendum' *together with what is below it towards about south*.

But, as noted before, the readers of Thucydides were not in our position, they knew less about the boundaries of the ancient city, and though they probably knew fairly well the limits of the Pelasgikon, even that was becoming rather a matter of antiquarian interest. Above all, they were citizens of the larger city of Themistocles, the Dipylon was more to them than the Enneapylon. Thucydides therefore feels that the truth about the ancient city needs driving home. He proceeds to give evidence for what was, he felt, scarcely self-evident. If we feel that the evidence is somewhat superfluous, we yet welcome it because incidentally he thereby gives us much and interesting information as to the sanctuaries of ancient Athens.

The evidence is, as above stated (p. 8), fourfold.

CHAPTER II.

THE SANCTUARIES IN THE CITADEL.

τὰ γὰρ ἱερὰ ἐν αὐτῇ τῇ ἀκροπόλει καὶ ἄλλων θεῶν ἐστί.

There are sanctuaries in the citadel itself, those of other deities as well (as The Goddess).

Needless difficulties have been raised about this sentence, and, quite unnecessarily, a lacuna in the text has been supposed[1]. Though the form of the sentence is compressed, the plain literal meaning is clear. The first piece of evidence that Thucydides states is that in the 'citadel itself other divinities "as well" have sanctuaries.' To what does this 'as well' refer? Obviously to 'The Goddess' mentioned in the clause next but one before as presiding over the Synoikia, 'The Goddess' who was so well known that to name her was needless.

It has been proposed to read the sentence thus: 'There are (ancient) sanctuaries in the citadel itself both "of the goddess Athena" and of other deities as well.' This is true, but it is not what Thucydides says and not what he means. He does not desire to make any statement whatever about the sanctuaries of Athene or their antiquity; both propositions are for the moment irrelevant; he *wishes* to say what he *does* say, that 'there are sanctuaries in the Acropolis itself, those of other deities as well (as The Goddess).' It is the 'other deities' not 'The Goddess' who are the point.

But Thucydides always leaves perhaps rather much to the intelligence of his readers. It may fairly be asked, why is the existence of these sanctuaries of 'other deities' an argument in support of the statement that the Acropolis was the ancient city?

[1] See Critical Note.

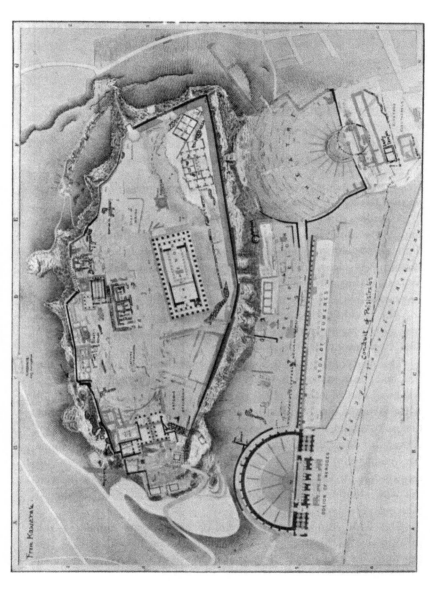

Fig. 16.

Once fairly asked, the question answers itself. The Acropolis in the time of Thucydides was a hill sacred to Athena, it was almost her *temenos*; the other gods, Apollo, Zeus, Aphrodite, had their most important sanctuaries down below, all over the great 'wheel-shaped' city. Athena had from time immemorial, it was believed, dwelt on the hill; any statement about her shrines would prove nothing one way or the other. But in the old days, before there was any 'down below,' any 'wheel-shaped' city, if the 'other gods' were to be city gods at all they must have their shrines up above. Such shrines there were on the Acropolis itself; this made it additionally probable that the Acropolis *was* the ancient city. The reasoning is quite clear and relevant, and the argument is just the sort that an Athenian of the time of Thucydides, with his head full of the dominant Athena, and apt to forget the 'other gods,' would need to have recalled to his mind.

The citadel of classical days, with its 'old Athena temple,' Parthenon and its Erechtheion lies before us in Fig. 16. The 'old Athena temple' and the Parthenon belong to 'The Goddess,' where then are the 'sanctuaries in the citadel itself which belong to other deities' of which Thucydides is thinking?

For such we naturally look to the north side of the Acropolis, where lay the ancient king's palace (Fig. 2, C). About that old palace westward there lay clustered a number of early altars, 'tokens' (σημεῖα), sacred places and things (ἱερά). Later these were enclosed in the complex building known to us as the Erechtheion. It is by studying the plan of this later temple that we can best understand the grouping and significance of the earlier sanctuaries.

The Erechtheion as we have it now is shown in Fig. 17. Its plan is obviously anomalous, and has puzzled generations of architects. It was reserved for Professor Dörpfeld, with his imaginative insight, to divine that the temple, as we have it, is incomplete; and, further, to reconstruct conjecturally the complete design. In the light of this reconstruction the Erechtheion, as we now possess it, became for the first time intelligible.

This reconstruction is shown in Fig. 18. The temple in the original plan was intended to consist of two cellas, each furnished with a pronaos; the east cella is marked on the plan 'Athena-

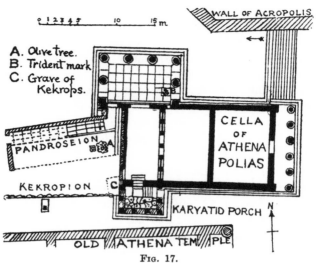

A. Olive tree.
B. Trident mark
C. Grave of Kekrops.

WALL OF ACROPOLIS

0 1 2 3 4 5   10   15 m.

PANDROSEION

KEKROPION

CELLA OF ATHENA POLIAS

C

KARYATID PORCH

N

OLD ATHENA TEMPLE

FIG. 17.

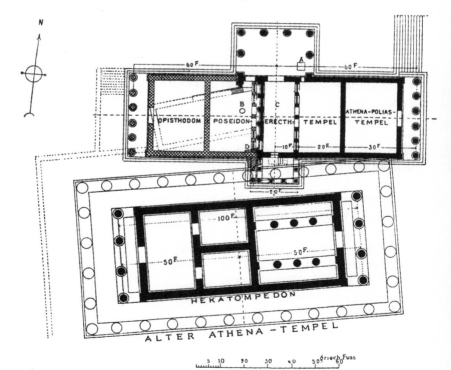

N

OPISTHODOM   POSEIDON-   ERECTH-TEMPEL   ATHENA-POLIAS-TEMPEL

60 F.   60 F.

A

B   C

D

10 F.   20 F.   30 F.

80 F.

100 F.

50 F.   50 F.

HEKATOMPEDON

ALTER ATHENA-TEMPEL

5   10   20   30   40   50   60   Griech. Fuss

FIG. 18.

Polias Tempel,' the west cella is marked 'opisthodom,' *i.e.* opisthodomos or back chamber. Between these two cellas is a building
divided into three chambers, marked in the plan 'Poseidon-
Erechth(eus)-Tempel.' The middle chamber of the three is
entered by two porches, a large one to the north, a smaller
one—the famous Karyatid porch—to the south. This middle
chamber alone of the three was probably provided with a low roof
as shown in the sketch in
Fig. 19. A building so
complex cries aloud for explanation. It has become
symmetrical, but what is
its significance? What for
us its connection with the
sanctuaries of 'other deities as well'?

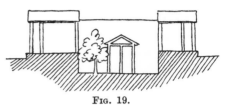

FIG. 19.

To understand the new temple we must go back to the times
before it was built[1]. It was intended—though ultimately this
intention was not fully accomplished—to replace other existing
sanctuaries, and these were first the old temple of Athena, and
second the old temple of Erechtheus. The 'old temple of Athena' appears on the plan (Fig. 18) to the south of the Erechtheion; the very
scanty remains of the old temple of Poseidon-Erechtheus are seen
running diagonally under the western part of the new Erechtheion.

The 'old temple of Athena' consisted, it is clear, of two parts:
to the east the actual cella of the goddess; to the west, divided
into three chambers, the opisthodomos or treasure-house. We
are concerned wholly, it must be noted, with the 'other deities,'
not with Athena; for from the consideration of Athena and her
sanctuaries Thucydides has dispensed us; but the arrangement
of the new Erechtheion cannot be understood without some
reference to the disposition of the old temple of Athena.

Perikles intended to demolish not only the old Erechtheion
but also the old temple of Athena, and to supplant them by a
common sanctuary. The east cella in the old Athena temple was
to be replaced by an east cella for the goddess in the new; the
opisthodomos to the west of the old temple by an opisthodomos
to the west of the new. Between these parts of the old Athena

---

[1] See throughout Prof. Dörpfeld, 'Der ursprüngliche Plan des Erechtheion,'
A. Mitt. 1904, p. 101, Taf. VI.

temple three chambers were to be devoted to replacing the old Erechtheion. It is difficult by help of ground-plans to realize the different levels of the temple, but those who have been on the spot will remember that the new cella of Athena is on the same level as the old. The Erechtheion with its different levels is a striking contrast to the Parthenon, where, as we have already seen, the slope of the ground was levelled up and that at enormous expense. This preservation of different levels in the Erechtheion is in itself sufficient evidence of the sanctity of the different cults to be enshrined. The longer complex structure, with its different levels and its five chambers, was intended, as Perikles planned it, to be entered by the two porches, north and south. Structurally these would reduce the effect of undue length, but they had also another purpose—the north porch contained the trident mark of Poseidon, the south the grave of Kekrops.

The plan of Perikles was never completed. By some one's machinations, whether of architect, priest, or politician we do not know, he was—as before in the building of the Propylaea— frustrated, and obliged to be content with a truncated scheme. The new Erechtheion almost certainly had been begun before the outbreak of the Peloponnesian War. When Perikles found that his plan was not accepted in full, he did not design a new temple but made a compromise obviously intended to be provisional. He was again frustrated in the execution even of this modified scheme, which was not completed till much later. The Erech-theion that we know has the east cella for Athena complete and the two porches, but two only of the three intended midway chambers were built, and the westernmost one, as appears on the plan, is slightly reduced in size. The west cella was never even begun. It is probable that Perikles never succeeded in trans-ferring the image of Athena from her old temple to the new cella, but this question[1] it is not necessary we should here decide.

Setting aside those portions of the Erechtheion which were intended to supply the place of the old temple of Athena, namely the east cella and the proposed opisthodomos to the west, we have now to consider what were the ancient sanctities ($\iota\epsilon\rho\acute{a}$) of

[1] See Dörpfeld, *A. Mitt.* xxviii. 1903, p. 468.

'other deities' which the three central chambers and the two porches were planned to enshrine. They are as follows:—

1. The hero-tomb of Kekrops.
2. The Pandroseion.
3. Three 'tokens' ($\sigma\eta\mu\epsilon\hat{\imath}a$).
    a. A sacred olive tree.
    b. A 'sea' called after Erechtheus.
    c. A trident mark sacred to Poseidon.

1. *The hero-tomb of Kekrops.*

We begin with Kekrops because, by almost uniform tradition, with Kekrops Athens began. The *Parian Chronicle*[1] sets him at the head of the kings of Athens, and the date assigned to him is 1582 B.C., before Kranaus, before Amphictyon, before Erechtheus. Thucydides[2] names him as the typical early Athenian king. 'Under Kekrops and the first kings,' he writes; Apollodorus[3] says definitely, 'the indigenous Kekrops, whose body was compounded of man and snake, first reigned over Attica, and the country which before was called Attica was from him named Kekropia.' Herodotus[4] looked back to a day before Athens was Athens and when there were no Athenians at all: 'The Athenians,' he says, 'at the time when the Pelasgians held that which is now called Hellas, were Pelasgians and they were called Kranai; under the rule of Kekrops they were called Kekropidae; but when Erechtheus succeeded they changed their name for that of Athenians, and when Ion, son of Xuthus, became general, they took from him the name of Ionians.'

Herodotus touches the truth. Kekrops was not the first king of *Athens*, he was king before there was any Athens, long before. He was the ancestor of the clan of the Kekropidae. At some very early date—the Parian marble may very likely be roughly right—the Kekropidae got possession of the Acropolis and called it Kekropia. Kekropis was the name not only of one of the four original Attic tribes but also of one of the later ten[5]. But though the clan kept its old name it lost the headship of Kekropia. Kekrops had only one son,

[1] ο]ντος Αθηνων Κεκροπος, ετη ΧΗΗΔ.   [2] Thucyd. II. 15.
[3] Apollod. III. 14.   [4] Herod. VIII. 44.
[5] Harp. *in voc.*; Poll. *On.* IX. 109.

Erysichthon[1], and he died childless; that is the mythological way
of saying that the kingship changed families. Then came the
time when the leading clan were Erechtheidae, descendants not
of Kekrops, but of Erechtheus. These are Homer's days. He
knows nothing of Kekrops and Kekropia, only of 'the people of
Erechtheus[2].' Then still later came another change; those who
once were the people of Erechtheus became the people of Athena,
Athenians. But Kekrops and Kekropia were first, probably long
first. Kekrops is the hero-founder, the typical old-world king.
It is Kekrops whom Bdelycleon[3], tormented by modernity,
invokes:

'Kekrops, oh my king and hero, thou that hast the dragon's feet.'

Kekrops was half man, half snake. His 'double nature' gave
logographers and even philosophers much trouble. Was it because
he had the understanding of a man and the strength of a dragon,
was it because, at first a good king, he later became a tyrant, or
because he knew two languages (Egyptian and Greek), or because
he instituted marriage? The curious will find it all in Tzetzes[4].
Eager anthropologists have seized on Kekrops as a totem-snake,
but the average orthodox mythologist is content to see in his
snake-tail the symbol of the 'earth-born' Athenians. This interpretation grazes the truth, but just misses the point. The hybrid
form is of course transitional. Kekrops is sloughing off his snake
form[5] in deference to the inveterate anthropomorphism of the
Greek. He was once a complete snake, not because he was a
totem-snake, not because he was an 'autochthonous hero,' but
because he was a dead man and all dead persons of importance,
all heroes, become snakes.

No one has done so much to obscure the early history of
Athenian religion as Athena herself, by her constant habit of
taking over the attributes of other divinities[6]. The eponymous

---

[1] Paus. i. 3. 6.   [2] Hom. *Il.* ii. 547 δῆμον Ἐρεχθῆος μεγαλητόρος.
[3] Aristoph. *Vesp.* 438 ὦ Κέκροψ ἥρως ἄναξ τὰ πρὸς ποδῶν δρακοντίδη.
[4] Tzetzes, *Chil.* v. 19.
[5] Only once so far as I know is Kekrops definitely called a snake, in the *Hekale*
of Callimachus; speaking of the decision in favour of Athene as against Poseidon
he says (v. 9)
τὴν ῥα νέον ψήφῳ (τ)ε Διὸς δύο καὶ δέκα τ' ἄλλων
ἀθανάτων ὄφιός τε κατέλλαβε μαρτυρίῃσιν.
See Gomperz, *Rainer Papyrus* vi. 1897, p. 9.
[6] Prof. Dörpfeld kindly suggests to me that the type of the Cretan Snake-
Goddess recently brought to light by Dr Evans and Miss Boyd may have had its

hero of each victorious tribe, Kekrops and Erechtheus in turn, is a home-keeping, home-guarding snake (οἰκουρὸς ὄφις). But by the time of Herodotus[1] the sacred snake supposed to live on and guard the Acropolis lives in the sanctuary of Athena, and is almost the embodiment of the goddess herself; when the snake refused the honey-cake it was taken as an omen that 'the goddess had deserted the Acropolis.' By the time of Pheidias the snake is just an attribute of the Parthenos, and was set to crouch beneath her shield. But Pausanias[2] has an inkling of the truth; he says, 'close beside the spear is a snake: this snake is probably Erichthonios.' The real relation of goddess and snake was simply this: the original pair of divinities worshipped in many local cults were a matriarchal goddess, a local form of earth-goddess, and the local hero of the place in snake form as her male correlative; such a pair were Demeter and the snake-king Kenchreus at Eleusis[3], such were Chryse and her home-keeping nameless guardian snake on Lemnos[4], such were Eileithyia and Sosipolis at Olympia[5], such were 'the goddess' and her successive heroes Kekrops and Erichthonios or Erechtheus; only, as will later be seen, in this last pair another goddess preceded Athena.

Kekrops then was a dead, divinized hero embodied as a snake; the natural place for his worship was his tomb, probably the earliest sanctuary of the Acropolis. Clement[6] of Alexandria says, 'the tomb of Kekrops is at Athens on the Acropolis,' and Theodoretus[7], quoting Antiochos, adds that it is 'by the Poliouchos herself,' the goddess of the city. We might safely assume that a hero-tomb was a sanctuary, but we have express evidence: in an honorary decree[8] respecting the 'ephebi' of the deme of Kekrops it is ordered that the decree shall be set up 'in the

---

influence on the goddess of Athens. I agree (see my *Prolegomena*, p. 307 note 3) and hope to return to this question on another occasion.

[1] Herod. VIII. 41. The snake was of course at first imaginary and Herodotus seems to doubt its existence.

[2] Paus. I. 24. 7.

[3] Hesiod. ap. Strab. IX. 9. § 393.

[4] Soph. *Philoct.* 1327.   [5] Paus. VI. 20. 2—4.

[6] Clem. Al. *Protr.* III. 45, p. 39.

[7] Theod. *Graec. affect. cur.* VIII. 30, p. 908 καὶ γὰρ Ἀθήνησιν, ὡς Ἀντίοχος ἐν τῇ ἐνάτῃ γέγραφεν ἱστορίᾳ ἄνω γε ἐν τῇ ἀκροπόλει Κέκροπός ἐστι τάφος παρὰ τὴν Πολιοῦχον αὐτήν.

[8] Δελτ. Ἀρχ. 1889, p. 10, fig. No. 3 ἐν τῷ τοῦ Κέκροπος ἱε[ρῷ.

sanctuary of Kekrops,' and from another decree [1] we learn the
name of a 'priest of Kekrops.'

But our most definite evidence as to where the tomb of
Kekrops lay comes from the famous Chandler inscription [2] now in
the British Museum. This inscription is exactly dated by the
archonship of Diokles (409–408 B.C.). It is a statement of the
exact condition in which the overseers of the unfinished temple
took over the work, what part was half finished, what unwrought
and unchannelled (*i.e.* columns), and what were completely finished
but not set up in their place. The various parts of the temple
are described as near or opposite to such and such an ancient
shrine, and fortunately among these descriptions occur more than
one mention of the Kekropion. The following [3] is decisive : 'Concerning the porch beside the Kekropion the roof stones above the
Korae must be....' The porch of the Karyatids, or to call it by its
ancient [4] name, the porch of the Korae, the Maidens, was beside,
close to, the Kekropion.

So far all is certain. The tomb of Kekrops was close to the
porch of the Maidens; but in which direction? We should
expect it to be north-west, because in that direction, as will be
immediately (p. 48) shown, lay the precinct of Pandrosos,
daughter of Kekrops. Professor Dörpfeld [5] places it conjecturally at
D (Fig. 16), and the site is almost certain. It has been already noted
that the west wall of the present Erechtheion was set back a short
distance within its original plan. It may have been to avoid
trenching on the tomb of Kekrops. Moreover, at the south end
of this wall there is a great gap in the ancient masonry of about
10 ft. long by 10 high. The gap is evident, though it was filled
up by modern masonry. It is spanned by an enormous ancient
block of stone, 15 ft. by 5. Here probably was buried the serpent
king.

[1] *C.I.A.* III. 1276 ἱε[ρ]εὺς Κέκρο[π]ος Ἀρίστων Σωσιστράτου Ἀθμονεύς.

[2] Brit. Mus. I. xxxv.; *C.I.A.* I. 322.   The inscription is engraved on two slabs of
Pentelic marble.

[3] *loc. cit.* line 83   ἐπὶ τἑι προστάσει τἑι πρὸς τὸ[ι]
Κεκροπίοι ἔδει
τὸς λίθος τὸς ὀροφιαίος τὸς
ἐπὶ τὸν κορὸν...

[4] For the name Caryatid as explained by Vitruvius see my *Mon. and Myth. Anc.
Athens*, p. 489.

[5] Dörpfeld, 'Der ursprüngliche Plan des Erechtheion,' *A. Mitt.* XXIX. p. 104,
1904.

With the serpent king and his
prophylactic tomb clearly in our
minds, we turn with new eyes to
examine certain fragments of sculpture discovered in the recent excavations. Nothing perhaps caused
more surprise when these fragments came to light than the size
and splendour of the snake-figures.
We have already seen (p. 27) that
the western pediment of the Hecatompedon held two sea-monsters,
a Triton and Typhon; the eastern
pediment held two land-snakes of
even greater magnificence. The
design of this pediment as restored by Dr. Wiegand[1] is as
follows (Fig. 19). In the apex is
seated Athena; to her right hand
a figure seated and crowned, and
therefore a king or a god; this
figure survives, but the figure which
must have balanced him to the left
of the goddess is lost for ever.
Athena is supreme; the surviving
figure is usually called Zeus, but
from his subordinate place it seems
to me that it is more likely he is
either a subordinate god, Poseidon,
or a local king, Erechtheus. Possibly Athena is seated between
Poseidon and Erechtheus.

It is, after all, not the seated
protagonists of the pediment, be
they Olympians or local kings, who
most interest us, but the two great

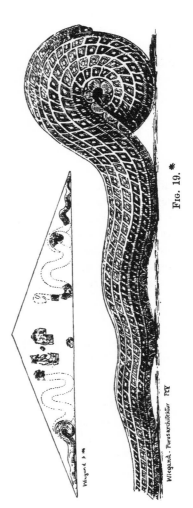

FIG. 19.

[1] Wiegand, *Die archäische Poros-Architektur der Akropolis zu Athen* (1904), p. 106;
and see also M. H. Lechat, *La sculpture
Attique avant Pheidias*, p. 53.

snakes who in the angles keep watch and ward. These snakes
are often described as 'decorative' or 'space-filling.' But
surely they are too alive, too large, too dominant to be mere
accessories. One of them is shown in Fig. 19*in detail, so far as
he can be represented by an uncoloured reproduction. In the
original he is blue and orange, and his companion in the other
angle is a vivid emerald green.

Herodotus[1], it is true, speaks of one snake only as guardian
of the Acropolis, the snake who when the land was beset by
the Persians, would not eat its honey-cake; but then Herodotus
writes as if he had no personal knowledge: 'the Athenians *say*
there is a great snake.' In the story of Erichthonios tradition,
and good Attic tradition, knew of two. Hermes in the *Ion* of
Euripides[2] says, referring to Erichthonios,

'To him
What time she gave him to the Agraulid maids
Athena bound for watch two guardian snakes;
In memory whereof Erechtheus' sons
In Athens still upon their nursing babes
Put serpents wrought of gold';

and on the well-known vase in the British museum[3] depicting the
scene, two snakes appear. We need not say that the two snakes
of the pediment are a duplicated Kekrops, but we may and do
say that they are two hero-snakes, guardians of the city, and we
may further *conjecture* that they were an old pair, male and
female. This conjecture brings us to the woman counterpart of
Kekrops, the snake king, his 'daughter' Pandrosos.

2. *The Pandroseion.*

Kekrops and his faithful daughter Pandrosos were not far
sundered. The situation of the Pandroseion is, within narrow
limits, certain. It was an enclosure to the west of the present

[1] Herod. vii. 41 λέγουσι Ἀθηναῖοι ὄφιν μέγαν φύλακα τῆς ἀκροπόλιος ἐνδιαιτᾶσθαι ἐν τῷ ἱρῷ.
[2] Eur. *Ion* 21—26, trans. Dr Verrall.
[3] Brit. Mus. Cat. E 418. See my *Myth. and Mon. Anc. Athens*, p. xxxi. Two snakes
also appear as Dr Wiegand *op. cit.* points out in the Atthis attributed to Amelesagoras;
see Westermann *Paradoxogr.* xii. 63 Ἀμελησαγόρας δὲ ὁ Ἀθηναῖος ὁ τὴν Ἀτθίδα
συγγράφων...φησὶ τὰς δὲ Κέκροπος θυγατέρας τὰς δύω Ἄγραυλον καὶ Πάνδροσον τὴν κίστην
ἀνοῖξαι καὶ ἰδεῖν δράκοντας δύω περὶ τὸν Ἐριχθόνιον. Hesychius *s.v.* οἰκουρὸς ὄφις says...
οἱ μὲν ἕνα φασὶν οἱ δὲ δύο ἐν τῷ ἱερῷ τοῦ Ἐρεχθέως.

Erechtheion. The invaluable Chandler inscription[1] speaks of 'the pillars on the wall towards the Pandroseion.' This must refer to the west wall, on which were four engaged pillars at a height of about 12 feet from the ground. In another inscription[2], found during the pulling down of the 'Odysseus' Bastion, mention is made of two pediments, one towards the east and the other 'towards the Pandroseion.'

We know, then, certainly that the Pandroseion was west of the present Erechtheion. We know also that it was close to the 'old temple of Athena.' Pausanias[3], in passing from the one to the other, distinctly says: 'The temple of Pandrosos adjoins the temple of Athena.' As Pausanias distinctly says there was a temple (ναός), not merely a temenos or sanctuary (ἱερόν), it is disappointing that excavations have yielded no trace.

In actual cultus and topography we have found Kekrops side by side with one woman figure, Pandrosos. In current mythology he has three daughters, of whom is told the thrice familiar story of the child and the chest[4]. It will repay examination.

The child Erichthonios is born from the Earth in the presence of Kekrops. His real mother, Earth, gives him up to the tendance of Athena; such is the scene familiar on terra-cottas and vase-paintings. Athena places him in a chest or wicker-basket, and gives him to the three daughters of Kekrops, Pandrosos, Herse, Aglauros, with strict orders not to open the chest. The two sisters, Herse and Aglauros (or according to some versions all three), overcome by curiosity open the chest, and see the child with a snake or snakes coiled about him. In terror at the snake, who pursues them, and fearing the anger of Athena, they cast themselves down from the Acropolis.

The story is manifestly absurd, and in some of the elements plainly aetiological.

The suicide of the disobedient sisters is easily explicable.

---

[1] *C.I.A.* I. 322, line 44
τὸν κίονον τὸν ἐπὶ τὸ τοίχο
τὸ πρὸς τὸ Πανδροσείο,
and in *C.I.A.* IV. 321, III. line 32
τὰ μετακιόνια τέτταρα ὄντα τὰ πρὸς τοῦ Πανδροσείου.

[2] Δελτ. Αρχ. 1888, p. 87, fig. 1 B, lines 27 and 41
ὁ πρὸς τοῦ Πανδροσείου.

[3] P. I. 27. 2 τῷ ναῷ δὲ τῆς Ἀθηνᾶς Πανδρόσου ναὸς συνεχής ἐστι.

[4] Paus. I. 18. 2. For the vase-paintings that illustrate the story see my *Myth. and Mon. Anc. Athens*, p. xxiii.

Half way down the Acropolis, below the steepest portion of the rock, were a number of shrines and tombs. Why were they there? Clearly because the persons after whom they were named had thrown themselves down, or been thrown down, from the top. Such a shrine was the tomb of Talos[1], near the Asklepieion. Daedalos was jealous of Talos, and threw him down from the rock. Such was also the shrine of Aegeus[2], below the temple of Nike Apteros, where Aegeus in despair at the sight of the black sail cast himself down. Such was the sanctuary of Aglauros[3] on the north side of the Acropolis. Somebody must have cast herself down to account for the situation. When one sister only is mentioned she is naturally Aglauros, but all three are often allowed to commit suicide for completeness sake.

Of the three sisters, Herse was not a real person[4]; she has no shrine, she is only a heroine invented to account for the ceremony of the Hersephoria. The cult of Aglauros is below the Acropolis and manifestly separate from that of Pandrosos, and Pandrosos alone for the present need be considered.

Pausanias, after stating that the temple of Pandrosos adjoins that of Athena, says that she was 'the only one of the sisters who was blameless in the affair of the chest intrusted to them.' As Pandrosos had a shrine so revered it would have been awkward to make her out guilty. He then, without telling us whether or no he perceives any connection, proceeds to describe 'a thing which caused me the greatest astonishment and is not generally known.' The thing that so astonished Pausanias was the ceremony of the Arrephoria[5]. Maidens called Arrephoroi bore upon their heads certain sacred things covered up; these they carried by night by a natural underground passage to a precinct near to that of Aphrodite in the Gardens. There they left what they had been carrying, and brought back other things also wrapped up and unknown. From the analogy of other mystery cults we may be sure that the objects carried were

---

[1] Paus. I. 21. 4 see *Myth. and Mon. Anc. Athens*, p. 299.
[2] P. I. 22. 5.   [3] P. I. 18. 2.
[4] See my 'Mythological Studies—the three daughters of Kekrops,' *Journ. Hell. Soc.* XII. p. 351, 1891.
[5] For a fuller discussion of the Arrephoria in relation to the Thesmophoria, see my *Prolegomena*, p. 131; and for the child in the mystery liknon, p. 525.

some sort of fertility-charms, and they would be carried in a chest or wicker basket, a *cista* or a *liknon*, veiled that the sacred thing might not be seen. The girl-Arrephoroi might not look into the sacred chests. Why? The answer was ready, the goddess they served, Pandrosos, had also her sacred chest into which she and she only had not looked.

The personality of Pandrosos is hard to seize and fix. One thing is clear; 'Pandrosos' is not a mere 'title of Athena.' She manifestly, as daughter of Kekrops, belongs to that earlier stratum before the dominance of The Goddess. Later Athena absorbed her as she absorbed everything else. In official inscriptions she usually comes after Athena, and is clearly a separate personality. Thus the epheboi[1] offered their 'sacrifices at departure ($\dot{\epsilon}\xi\iota\tau\dot{\eta}\rho\iota\alpha$) on the Acropolis to Athena Polias and to Kourotrophos and to Pandrosos,' and women swore by her, though not so often as by Aglauros. We have one ritual particular that looked as though between her and Athene there was at some time friction. Harpocration[2] in explaining the rare word '$\dot{\epsilon}\pi\iota\beta\sigma\iota\sigma\nu$,' 'that which is after the ox,' says, quoting from Philochoros, that it was the name given to a sacrifice to Pandrosos. If any one sacrificed an ox to Athena it was necessary to sacrifice a sheep to Pandrosos. Pandrosos was in danger of being effaced by Athena, and some one was determined this should not be; all that 'The Goddess' could secure was precedence.

We have found, then, a maiden goddess who was there before 'The Goddess,' nay, who may have herself been 'The Goddess' before Athena claimed the title. Pandrosos belongs to the early order of the Kekropidae, before the dwellers on the hill became Athenians. It is possible that her presence throws some light on the beautiful, but as yet enigmatic figures of the 'Maidens' who have been restored to us by the recent excavations. Who and what are they?

The 'Maiden' whose figure is chosen for the frontispiece of this book was found alone, somewhat later than the rest, in October, 1888, not like the others (p. 16) North of the Erechtheion, but near the wall of Kimon to the South, between the precinct of Artemis-Brauronia and the West front of the Parthenon. There

[1] *C.I.A.* II. 481, 58.   [2] s.v. $\dot{\epsilon}\pi\iota\beta\sigma\iota\sigma\nu$.

is a certain fitness in this, because though in dress, adornments, colouring, general type, she is like the rest, her great beauty will always make her a thing apart. The torso and head were found separate, and about the torso there is nothing specially noteworthy. The unique loveliness is all of the face, and it escapes analysis. There are, however, peculiarities worth noting. The right eye is set much more obliquely than the left. This gives an irregular charm and individuality; the unusually high forehead emphasizes the austere virginal air, and the same may be said of the straight chest and long thin throat. But the secret of her beauty is still kept; standing as she does now among the other 'Maidens,' she is a creature from another world, and for all their beauty the rest look but a kindly mob of robust mothers and genial housewives.

The statues in question, which now number upwards of fifty, have been called by the name 'Maidens,' a name current among archaeologists. It is open to objection, because 'maidens' (κόραι) meant in the official language of the inscription already quoted[1] the 'Caryatid' figures of the Erechtheion. The word has, however, one great advantage, it is vague and commits the user of it to no theory as to the significance of the statues. The word *korè* meant to the Greek not only maiden, but doll or puppet or statue of a maiden. We need only recall the familiar epigram with the dedication to Artemis[2]:

> Maid of the Mere, Timaretè here brings
>   Before she weds, her cymbals, her dear ball
> To thee a Maid, her maiden offerings,
>   Her snood, her maiden dolls their clothes and all.

Here the *korai* are actual *dolls*, but in Attic inscriptions we find the word *korè* used of a statue[3], thus, 'a korè of gold on a pillar'; or again in a dedication to Poseidon, 'he dedicated as firstfruits this *korè*.' A *korè* is one form of an *agalma*, a thing of delight.

The statues, then, may be called 'Maidens,' but the word is too vague to help us much as to their significance, and it is their

---

[1] *C.I.A.* I. 322 (Brit. Mus. I. 35. 571), l. 83 ἐπὶ τει προστάσει τει πρὸς τὸ[ι] Κεκροπίοι ἔδει τὸς λίθος τὸς ὀροφιαίος τὸς ἐπὶ τὸν κορὸν ἐπεργάσασθαι ἄνοθεν, see p. 46.

[2] *Anth. Pal.* VI. 280
τάς τε κόρας Λιμνᾶτι Κόρα κόρα, ὡς ἐπιεικὲς
ἄνθετο·
see my *Prolegomena*, p. 301.

[3] *C.I.A.* I. 141 κορὴ χρυσῆ ἐπὶ στήλης, v. Lolling, *Cat. des inscr. de l'Acropole*, No. 267 τήνδε κόρην ἀνέθηκεν ἀπαρχήν.

significance, who and what they are, not their value in the history of art that here concerns us.

The question is generally put thus, Are they statues of Athena, or are they statues of mortal women dedicated to her? priestesses or merely worshippers? Statues of Athena they are, I think, certainly *not*; they have neither helmet, spear, shield, nor even aegis. Athena may appear sporadically without characteristic attributes, but that a series of fifty statues of Athena should be dedicated without a single hint of anything that made Athena to be Athena is scarcely possible.

Are they, then, mortal maidens? For priestesses their number, restricted as they are by style to a short period of years, is too many. If they are mere mortal worshippers, it is at least strange that in the only two cases where we have inscribed bases they are dedicated by men. In one case we have the simple statement: 'Euthydikos son of Thalearchus dedicated[1]'; on the other, Antenor, it is stated, makes the statue, Nearchos dedicates it as 'firstfruits of his works[2].' Would Nearchos dedicate a statue of mortal woman as 'firstfruits of his works'? We seem to be at an *impasse*.

But there is surely a third solution open to us. The maidens need not be mortal because they are not Athena. There was a time before the armed maiden with spear and shield and aegis came from Libya or the East, a time when another maiden ruled upon the hill and was 'The Goddess.' Is it not at least possible that the maidens are made in her image, and that when the armed goddess took possession of the hill, when the ancient Kekropidae and Erechtheidae became Athenaioi, the maidens of the old order passed into the service of the maiden of the new? that we must think of their type as shaped at least for the worship of Pandrosos rather than Athena? The type of the warlike goddess was not fashionable in Greece. The Greeks, if any people, held firmly the doctrine that

A woman armed makes war upon herself.

The woman armed and disarmed, the Amazon in defeat, they made beautiful and poignantly human, but the woman armed

[1] *Jahrbuch d. Inst.* II. 1887, p. 219.
[2] *C.I.A.* IV. suppl. 373 and *Eph. Arch.* 1886, p. 81, l. 6.

and triumphant, Athena Nikephoros, remained a cold unreality. The *korè* of Eleusis is not armed, but at Corinth and at Sparta there was that strangest of all sights—the image of Aphrodite armed [1]. Whence she came is, as will later be seen (p. 109), not doubtful. In Cythera [2], Pausanias tells us, 'the sanctuary of the Heavenly Goddess is most holy, and of all Greek sanctuaries of Aphrodite this is most ancient. The goddess is represented by a wooden image armed.' The Cythereans called their armed Oriental goddess Cytherea. Did the Athenians call the same armed goddess 'Athenaia'? Be that as it may, before her coming they worshipped the *un*armed maiden.

Before we pass from Kekrops and Pandrosos to the later order under Erechtheus, the traditional events reputed of the reign of Kekrops must be noted. There are three :—

1. The contest between Athena and Poseidon, of which Kekrops acted as judge.
2. The introduction of the worship of Zeus.
3. The institution of marriage.

The discussion of the contest between Athena and Poseidon really belongs to the Erechtheid period, and must stand over till then. The introduction of the worship of Zeus and the institution of marriage are probably but the religious and social forces of the same advance, and may be taken together.

In front of the Erechtheion, Pausanias [3] tells us, was an altar dedicated to Zeus Hypatos, on which no living thing was sacrificed, but only cakes ($\pi\acute{\epsilon}\lambda\alpha\nu\omicron\iota$). Pausanias does not here say that the altar was dedicated by Kekrops, but, in his discussion of Arcadia [4] and the human sacrifice of Lycaon, he says, 'Kekrops was the first who gave to Zeus the title of Supreme, and he would not sacrifice anything that had life, but he burned on the altar the local cakes which the Athenians to this day call *pelanoi*.' What probably happened was just the reverse of what Pausanias describes: there was an old altar to 'the Supreme,' the *Hypatos*; at some time or other this was taken over by the immigrant Zeus; the shift was attributed to Kekrops.

[1] Paus. ii. 5. 1, iii. 15. 10.   [2] Paus. iii. 21. 10.
[3] Paus. i. 26. 5.   [4] Paus. viii. 2. 3.

Zeus was essentially of the patriarchal order, *i.e.* of a condition of things in which the father rather than the mother is the head of the family, gives his name to the children, and holds the family property and conducts the family worship. Nothing could be more patriarchal than the constitution of the Homeric Olympus. Such a condition of things is necessarily connected with some form of the social institution known to us as marriage. Accordingly we learn from Athenaeus[1], quoting from Clearchus the pupil of Aristotle, that 'At Athens Kekrops was the first to join one woman to one man: before connections had taken place at random and marriages were in common—hence as some think Kekrops was called "Twyformed" ($\delta\iota\phi\upsilon\dot{\eta}\varsigma$), since before his day people did not know who their fathers were on account of the number' (of possible parents). The story of the contest between Athene and Poseidon was later mixed up with the same tradition of the shift from patriarchy to matriarchy. St Augustine[2] says that the women voted for Athena, and their punishment was to be, among other things, that 'no one was hereafter to be called by his mother's name.'

We pass to the three tokens ($\sigma\eta\mu\epsilon\hat{\iota}a$), the first of which is

a. The sacred olive-tree.

> The holy bloom of the olive, whose hoar leaf
> High in the shadowy shrine of Pandrosos
> Hath honour of us all.

Apollodorus[3] says, 'After him (Poseidon) came Athena, and having made Kekrops witness of her seizure, she planted the olive which is now shown in the Pandroseion.' A 'seizure' indeed, and not from Poseidon but from the elder goddess Pandrosos. Athena is manifestly an interloper; why should Pandrosos have other people's olive trees planted in *her* precinct? The olive is but one of the many 'tokens' or attributes that Athena wrested to herself. It was there before her, Kekrops quite rightly holds it in his hand.

The olive-tree grew in the Pandroseion, it also grew in the older Erechtheion. Herodotus[4] says, 'There is on this Acropolis

---

[1] Athen. XIII. 2. § 555 and Tzetzes, *Chil.* v. 19. v. 650.
[2] S. Aug. *de civitat. Dei*, 18. 9 ut nullus nascentium maternum nomen acciperet.
[3] Apollod. III. 14. 2 μετὰ δὲ τοῦτον ἧκεν Ἀθηνᾶ, καὶ ποιησαμένη τῆς καταλήψεως Κέκροπα μάρτυρα ἐφύτευσεν ἐλαίαν ἣ νῦν ἐν τῷ Πανδροσείῳ δείκνυται.
[4] Herod. VIII. 55.

a temple of Erechtheus, who is called earth-born, and in it are an olive-tree and a sea which, according to the current tradition among the Athenians, Poseidon and Athenaia planted as tokens when they contended for the country.' There is no discrepancy, the Pandroseion must have been included in the older Erechtheion.

By a most happy chance, among the fragments of decorative sculpture left us is one on which is carved 'the holy bloom of the olive,' in three delicate sprays. The real sacred olive was old and stunted and crooked[1], but the artist went his own way. The fragments are grouped together in a conjectural restoration[2] in Fig. 20. All that is certain is that we have a Doric building and adjacent to it the wall of a precinct over which the olive is growing. Against the wall of the building is the figure of a woman in purple, wearing peplos and himation. Against the wall of the precinct once stood a man. Only one leg of him is left. The two figures might be part of a procession. The woman, standing full face, *may* belong to the same composition, but this is not certain. She wears a red chiton and bluish-green himation. On her head is a pad (τύλη), for she is carrying some burden. One of her arms is lifted to support it. We think instinctively of the Arrephoroi. The figure, though very rudely hewn, has something of the lovely seriousness of the other 'maidens.' The whole composition may have belonged to a pediment of the earlier Erechtheion, but its pictorial character makes it more probably a votive relief for dedication there, and representing some scene of worship at the ancient shrine.

Within the older Erechtheion we have further

(*b*) A cistern or 'sea,' called after Erechtheus. With it may be taken

(*c*) A trident-mark, sacred to Poseidon.

Fortunately about the position of these two sacred things there is no doubt. Underneath the pavement of the westernmost chamber (*c*) of the present Erechtheion is a large cistern[3] hewn

---

[1] Hesych. Fig. 146 ἀστὴ ἐλαία, ἡ ἐν ἀκροπόλει ἡ καλουμένη παγκύφος διὰ χθαμαλότητα.

[2] For full discussion of the fragments see Dr Th. Wiegand, *Die archäische Poros-Architektur der Akropolis zu Athen*, p. 97; *Das älteste Erechtheion und der heilige Oelbaum*, Taf. xiv. on which the restoration in Fig. 20 is based. The door really at the *end* of the building is, perhaps by a not uncommon convention, brought into view at the *side*. Cf. the temple of Janus on a coin of Nero.

[3] Unfortunately the site of the 'sea' has never been systematically excavated

Temple of Janus from Coin of Nero.

Fig. 20.

in the rock, and at A in the North porch are the marks of the trident.

The two things together, the sea-water in the cistern and the trident-mark, were both associated with Poseidon. Pausanias[1] says they were said to be 'the evidence produced by Poseidon in support of his claim to the country.' Apollodorus[2] says, 'Poseidon came first to Attica and smote with his trident in the middle of the Acropolis and produced the sea which they now call Erechtheïs.'

Athena produced the olive-tree, Poseidon the salt well and the trident-mark as 'tokens' or evidence of their claim. This is manifest aetiology. There had been on the Acropolis from time immemorial certain things reputed sacred, a gnarled olive-tree, a brackish well, three holes in a rock. It was the obvious policy of any divinity who wished to be worshipped at Athens to annex these tokens. Pandrosos had the olive-tree before Athena. The name of the well Erechtheïs shows that it was a 'token' of Erechtheus rather than of Poseidon.

Such sacred trees, such 'seas,' such curious marks existed elsewhere; Pausanias[3] himself notes in another inland place, Aphrodisias in Caria, there was a sea-well. What impressed him as noteworthy about the well at Athens was that when the South wind was blowing it gave forth the sound of waves, but then as he does not say if he waited for a South wind, the 'sound of waves' may have been a detail supplied by the guides.

The trident-mark belongs to a class of sacred things that will repay somewhat closer attention. Fresh light has been thrown upon it by a recent discovery. In examining the roof of the North Porch, with a view to repairs, it was observed that immediately above the trident-mark an opening in the roof had been purposely left. The object is clear; the sacred token had to be left

and examined. Professor Dörpfeld tells me that the cistern now visible is of mediaeval date. Until the mediaeval masonry is removed the precise character of the 'sea' cannot be determined. There was certainly no *spring*, the geological character of the Acropolis plateau forbids that, but a *well* may exist.

[1] Paus. I. 26. 5 ταῦτα δὲ λέγεται Ποσειδῶνι μαρτύρια ἐς τὴν ἀμφισβήτησιν τῆς χώρας φανῆναι.

[2] Apollod. III. 14. 1.

[3] Paus. I. 26. 5. The sea well at Caria was sacred to a foreign god called Osogoa, see Paus. VIII. 10. 4. It is worth noting that Semitic gods have 'seas' in their sanctuaries; Solomon's temple had a brazen 'sea' and Marduk at Babylon had a *tamtu* or sea, and curiously enough it was associated with the great serpent. See King, *Babylonian Religion*, p. 105.

open to the sky; it had to be *sub divo*. This is manifestly more appropriate to a sky-god than to a sea-god.

Our best analogies are drawn from Roman sources. Ovid[1] tells us that when the new Capitol was being built a whole multitude of divinities were consulted by augury as to whether they would withdraw to make place for Jupiter. They tactfully consented, all but old Terminus. He stood fast, remaining in his shrine, and still possesses a temple in common with mighty Jupiter:

> And still, that he may see only heaven's signs
> In the roof above him is a little hole.

When place was wanted for an Olympian, be he Zeus or Poseidon or Athena, the elder divinities were not always so courteously consulted. We do not even know whose open air token Poseidon seized.

Servius[2], commenting on 'the steadfast stone of the Capitol,' tells the same story. There was a time when there was no temple of Jupiter, that is there was no Jupiter. Augury said that the Tarpeian mount was the place to build one, but on it were already a number of shrines of other divinities. Ceremonies were performed to 'call out' by means of sacrifice the other divinities to other temples. They all willingly migrated, only Terminus declined to move: this was taken as a sign that the Roman empire would be for all eternity, and hence in the Capitoline temple the part of the roof immediately above, which looks down on the very stone of Terminus, was open, *for to Terminus it is not allowable to sacrifice save in the open air*. Terminus was just a sacred stone or herm, incidentally to the practical Romans a boundary god. Another Roman god, Fidius[3], had in his temple a roof with a hole in it (perforatum tectum), and Fulgur, Caelum, Sol and Luna had all to dwell in hypaethral temples[4]. Wherever the lightning struck was in Greece holy ground, to be fenced in but open always above to the god who had sanctified it, to the 'descender,' Kataibates[5]. Kataibates became Zeus Kataibates, Fulgur Jupiter Fulgur, but the lightning and the 'descender'

---

[1] Ovid *Fasti*, ii. 667
Nunc quoque, se supra ne quid nisi sidera cernat
Exiguum templi tecta foramen habent.
[2] Serv. *ad Aen.* ix. 448.
[3] Varro *L. L.* v. 66. [4] Vitr. i. 2. 5. [5] Paus. v. 14. 10.

were there before the coming of the Olympian, and the threefold mark preceded Poseidon.

In picturing to ourselves therefore the ancient sanctities of the Acropolis, we have to begin with certain natural holy things that were there from time immemorial, that were holy in themselves, not because they were consecrated to this or that divinity. Such were the olive-tree, the salt sea-well, the trident-mark—we are back in a time rather of holy things than divine persons. Successive heroic families, in possessing themselves of the kingship, take possession of these sanctities ; they are as it were the regalia. In the time of the Kekropidae, Pandrosos, daughter and *paredros* of Kekrops, owns the olive-tree; in the time of the Erechtheidae the well is called Erechtheïs, and all the sacred things are included in an Erechtheion. It is worth noting that though Poseidon claimed the well and the trident-mark he never gave his name to either, and though Athena boasted of the olive-tree and snake, neither was ever called after her.

The name of Erechtheus or Erechthonios marks a stage definitely later than that of Kekrops. In the reign of Kekrops we hear nothing of foreign policy. He is engaged in civilizing his people, in marrying them, in teaching them to offer bloodless sacrifice. But the reign of Erechtheus is marked by a great war. He fought with and conquered Eumolpos, king of the neighbouring burgh Eleusis. Kekropia has taken the first step towards that hegemony she was to obtain under Theseus.

Erechtheus, not Kekrops, is the king-hero known to Homer ; the two passages in which he and his city are mentioned are significant. In the *Odyssey*[1], Athena, having counselled Odysseus, leaves him to make his entrance alone into the house of Alkinoös, while she betakes herself home. 'Therewith grey-eyed Athene departed over the unharvested seas and left pleasant Scheria and came to Marathon and wide-wayed Athens, and entered the good house of Erechtheus.' Here manifestly Athena has no temple, she has to shelter herself in the good house of Erechtheus ('Ερεχθῆος πυκινὸν δόμον). That is how it used to be in the old kingly days, the king was divine, his palace a sanctuary.

But in the Catalogue of the Ships[2]—allowed on all hands to

---

[1] *Od.* vii. 80—81, trans. Butcher and Lang.   [2] *Il.* ii. 546.

be a later document—things are quite otherwise. Among the captains of the ships were 'they that possessed the goodly citadel of Athens, the domain of Erechtheus the high-hearted, whom erst Athene, daughter of Zeus, fostered, when Earth, the grain-giver, brought him to birth;—and she gave him a resting-place in Athens, in her own rich sanctuary; and there the sons of the Athenians worship him with bulls and rams as the years turn in their courses.'

The passage is a notable one. The singer is manifestly in some difficulty. Athena by his time is supreme; she has a goodly temple: it is she who offers hospitality to Erechtheus, not Erechtheus to her. Yet the singer knows the early tradition that the goodly citadel belongs to the king Erechtheus, he also knows the ritual fact that annual sacrifice was offered to him. This ritual fact of the sacrifice to Erechtheus is attested by Herodotus[1]. He tells us that the Epidaurians were allowed to cut down sacred olive-trees to make statues from, on the express condition that they annually sacrificed victims to Athena Polias and Erechtheus. Here the goddess joins in the honours, a fact not expressly stated in Homer, though probably understood.

So far we have Erechtheus, hero-king, snake-king, like the earlier Kekrops and Athena. Athena, it is evident, is the later intruder, but we have had no evidence of Poseidon. Poseidon's position at Athens is a very peculiar one. Unlike Erechtheus, he has no temple called after him, he cannot give his name even to a salt sea-well, his trident-mark is probably to begin with a thunder-smitten rock; unlike Athena he never gets the people called after him, and yet, spite of all this, his worship is ancient and deep-rooted, and from him rather than from Zeus or Athena the old nobility of Athens claimed to be descended.

We are so accustomed to regard Athena as the Alpha and well-nigh the Omega of Athenian religion that the priority of Poseidon, one of the 'other gods,' needs emphasis. The Athenians themselves, however, at least the more conservative[2] among them, recognized it. Poseidon they knew was son of Kronos, and Athena daughter only of the younger Zeus.

'O Sea-Poseidon and ye elderly gods'

[1] Herod. v. 82.
[2] For Poseidon as the Tory-god I am indebted to Mr R. A. Neil's edition of the *Knights*; see lines 144 and 551.

exclaims the youth in the *Plutus* when he holds the torch to the
wrinkles in the old woman's withered face.   When, in the *Frogs*,
Euripides is made to utter what is taken to be a fine old conservative sentiment, Dionysos answers 'Good by Poseidon, that!'
When in the *Knights* Nicias the household slave—conservative
after the manner of his class—hears that the new demagogue
is a black-pudding chandler, he exclaims in horror,

'A black-pudding chandler, Poseidon what a trade!'

The choice of Poseidon by the conservative party was no mere
chance; they believed in him, they swore by him, because they
thought they were descended from him.   In the case of one noble
family, the Butadae, this descent was no mere chance tradition;
their family tree was written up in the Erechtheion itself, and they
claimed to be descended from a certain Butes, son of Poseidon and
brother of Erechtheus.   When Pausanias[1] entered the later
Erechtheion he saw in the first chamber three altars, 'one sacred
to Poseidon on which sacrifices are offered to Erechtheus in
accordance with the command of an oracle, one to the hero Butes,
and one to Hephaestos; the paintings on the wall represent the
family of the Butadae.'   It is often said that Erechtheus is merely
a 'title' of Poseidon; this was the view of the lexicographers.
Hesychius[2] explains Erechtheus as 'Poseidon at Athens.'   But the
statement about the altar shows that they were *not* originally the
same, the command of an oracle was needed to affiliate them.   It
is a noticeable point moreover that Poseidon has no temple of his
own, only an altar in the 'dwelling' (οἴκημα) called the Erechtheion.
This sanctuary bearing the kingly name, remains his 'steadfast
house' and is an eternal remembrance of the days when the king
was priest and the god's vicegerent on earth.

But there came a time when kings ceased to be in the old full
sense incarnate gods, and then the kingly function was split into
two offices, secular and spiritual.   Of this at Athens we have
traces in the narrative of Apollodorus[3].   He says 'on the death of
Pandion his sons divided the paternal estate and Erechtheus
took the kingship, but Butes took the priesthood of Athena and
of Poseidon the son of Erechthonios.   It was the family tree of the

[1] Paus. I. 26. 5.
[2] s.v. Ἐρέχθευς, but the scholiast in Lycophron, *Al.* 431, says Ἐρέχθευς ὁ Ζεὺς ἐν
Ἀθήναις καὶ ἐν Ἀρκαδίᾳ τιμᾶται; see Mr A. B. Cook, *Classical Review*, 1904, p. 85.
[3] Apollod. III. 15. 1.

royal priest Butes that was religiously preserved in the Erechtheion. The 'paintings' on the wall could of course only go back to the rebuilding of those walls in 409 B.C., but the genealogical tree would go back to time immemorial. In the *Lives of the Ten Orators*[1] we hear of Lycurgus, the Eteobutad, as follows. His ancestors derived from Erechtheus, son of Ge and Hephaestos, but his immediate ancestors were Lycomedes and Lycurgus, whom the people had honoured with a public funeral. And the descent of his family from those who held office as priests of Poseidon is on a complete tablet in the Erechtheion written up by Ismenios son of Chalcideus and there are wooden images of Lycurgos and his sons, of Habron, Lycurgos and Lycophron made by Timarchos and Cephisodotos the son of Praxiteles. And Habron dedicated the tablet to his son, and coming in succession to the priesthood he resigned in favour of his brother Lycophron. Hence Habron is represented handing over the trident to him.

By such family trees, by the genealogies and successive priesthoods of royal priestly families, was ancient chronology kept. Argive chronology it will be remembered was reckoned by the years of the consecration of the successive priestesses of Hera[2]. The record was kept in the ancient sanctuary of the Heraion and the statues of the priestesses were set up in front of the temple[3].

With the question of the cult of Athena we have not to deal, but as Poseidon is emphatically one of the 'other gods' a word must be said about the subordinate position he comes to occupy. This position is remarkable. To the conservative party as we have seen he was a god of the first importance; it is very noticeable that the chorus of Knights[4] sing first to 'Poseidon lord of horses' and only second to 'Pallas, She of the Citadel.' Their normal orthodox relation, Athena first, Poseidon second, is reflected in the hymn at Colonos. Yet when we come to examine the ritual of the two divinities we find that their priesthood was conjoint; the Butadae held the priesthood not only of Poseidon but of Athena[5].

These difficulties, these incongruities in tradition, would no

[1] *Vit. X. Orat.* p. 843°.   [2] Thucyd. II. 2.
[3] Paus. II. 17. 3. For the whole subject of the importance of these priestly genealogies, see Professor Ridgeway, *Early Age of Greece*, p. 102.
[4] Aristoph. *Eq.* 551. See Mr R. A. Neil, *ad loc.*
[5] Apollod. III. 15. 1. See *supra*, p. 62.

doubt be easily solved did we fully know the origin of the cults of Poseidon and Athena. This at present is hidden from our eyes. Kekrops, Pandrosos, Erechtheus, are obviously local. Their worship never spread beyond the hill of Athens, but Poseidon and Athena were worshipped over the whole of Hellas, and whether in Athens they were indigenous or imported cannot at present be certainly said. Herodotus[1] emphatically states that Poseidon originated in Libya, 'for none except the Libyans originally possessed the name of Poseidon and they have always worshipped him.' It is in Libya also that this same Herodotus[2] notes that the dwellers round lake Tritonis sacrifice principally to Athena and next to Triton and Poseidon, and from the Libyan women the Greeks obtained the dress and the aegis of the statues of Athena.

If we may hazard a glimpse into things remote or dark, it may be conjectured that the worship of Poseidon and Athena came from Libya to Attica from a people geographically remote, but with racial affinities[3]. That in Libya Athena was, as Herodotus notes, the more important of the two. An old matriarchal goddess, transplanted to Athens in the days of king Erechtheus, she fell when social conditions were patriarchal rather than matriarchal to a subordinate place. Poseidon rather than Athena stood at the head of the Athenian family trees. He headed the conservative aristocratic party. But at some time of political upheaval, possibly even as late as the time of Peisistratos[4], the tide turned, and the ancient matriarchal goddess, as patron of the tyrants and the democracy, reasserted herself. It is Athena not Poseidon who brings Peisistratos back in her chariot to Athens. All this, the prior supremacy of Poseidon, the resurgence of Athena, is reflected in the myth of the *Eris*, the rivalry, the contest of the two divinities for the land, in the aetiological myth of the planting of the olive-tree and the smiting of the rock with the trident.

To resume, among the 'other deities' are first and foremost Kekrops and Erechtheus, ancient eponymous kings, Pandrosos the daughter and *paredros* of Kekrops and later affiliated to these the

---

[1] Herod. ii. 50. See R. Brown, *Poseidon*, 1872, p. 66.   [2] Herod. iv. 188—189.
[3] See Prof. Ridgeway, *The Early Age of Greece*, p. 226.
[4] Herod. i. 59. To the question of the origin and development of the cult of Athena and to the examination of certain Oriental factors in it I hope to return on another occasion.

immigrant Poseidon. Their 'sacred things' are the tomb of
Kekrops, the olive, the 'sea,' the trident-mark. The list does not
exhaust the 'other deities' worshipped on the Acropolis; Zeus
had altars, Artemis perhaps from early days a precinct. Herakles,
though probably an oriental immigrant, was worshipped on the
Acropolis at a very early date. It has been one of the sudden
corrections sometimes so sharply administered by archaeology to
our prejudice that, among the ancient poros sculptures of which
so many remains have come to light, Herakles is prominent,
Theseus conspicuously absent. But the group of deities and
sanctities that cluster round the Erechtheion are sufficient for
our purpose, and for that of Thucydides. They show that the
Acropolis was the *polis* for the simple reason that '*there are
sanctuaries in the citadel itself, those of other deities as well* (as
the Goddess).

CHAPTER III.

THE SANCTUARIES THAT ARE OUTSIDE THE CITADEL.

καὶ τὰ ἔξω πρὸς τοῦτο τὸ μέρος τῆς πόλεως μᾶλλον ἵδρυται, τό τε τοῦ Διὸς τοῦ
'Ολυμπίου καὶ τὸ Πύθιον καὶ τὸ τῆς Γῆς καὶ τὸ ἐν Λίμναις Διονύσου (ᾧ τὰ ἀρχαιότερα
Διονύσια τῇ δωδεκάτῃ ποιεῖται ἐν μηνὶ 'Ανθεστηριῶνι) ὥσπερ καὶ οἱ ἀπ' 'Αθηναίων "Ιωνες
ἔτι καὶ νῦν νομίζουσιν, ἵδρυται δὲ καὶ ἄλλα ἱερὰ ταύτῃ ἀρχαῖα.

THUCYD. II. 15.

LET us recapitulate. Thucydides has made a statement as to
the city before the days of Theseus.—*Before this, what is now the
citadel was the city, together with what is below it towards about
South.* In support of this statement he has adduced one argument.
*The sanctuaries are in the Citadel itself, those of other deities as
well (as the Goddess).* He now adduces a second, '*And those that
are outside are placed towards this part of the city more (than elsewhere). Such are the sanctuary of Zeus Olympios, and the Pythion,
and the sanctuary of Ge, and that of Dionysos-in-the-Marshes (to
whom is celebrated the more ancient Dionysiac Festival on the 12th
day in the month Anthesterion, as is also the custom down to the
present day with the Ionian descendants of the Athenians); and
other ancient sanctuaries also are placed there.*

This second argument we have now to examine :—

By '*this part of the city*' it is quite clear that Thucydides
means that portion of the city of his own day which he has
carefully marked out; *i.e.* the citadel *plus* something, *plus* '*what
is below it towards about South*'; by this we have seen is meant
the upper citadel *plus* the Pelargikon. This second piece of
evidence is, like the first, adduced simply to prove the small limits
of the ancient city. But Thucydides has expressed himself somewhat carelessly. Readers who did not know where the sanctuaries
adduced as instances were, might and have taken '*towards this*

part of the city' to mean *'towards about South.'* The proximity of
the two phrases and the appearance of a relation between them,
if in fact there be no relation is, as Dr Verrall[1] observes, 'a flaw in
composition which would not have been passed by a pupil of
Isocrates.' The carelessness of Thucydides is, however, excusable
enough. He assumes that the position of the shrines he instances
is known as it was by every Athenian of his day. He also assumes
that the main gist of his argument is intelligently remembered,
that his readers realize that he is concerned with the character
and *dimensions* not the *direction* of his ancient city.

All that Thucydides tells us is that the sanctuaries outside the
ancient city are *'towards'* it[2]: strictly speaking he gives us absolutely no information as to whether they are North, South, East or
West. But *'towards' implies* approach, and, if we are told that
sanctuaries are *'towards'* a place, we naturally think of ourselves
as going there and as finding these sanctuaries on and about the
approach to that place.

As to the direction of the approach to the Acropolis there is
happily no manner of doubt. In Thucydides' own days it was
where it now is, due West; in the days before the Persian War, the
days when the old sanctuaries grew up towards the approach, it
was South-West. We know then roughly where to look for our
'outside' sanctuaries; they will be about the entrance West and
South-West. We must however remember that the whole ancient
entrance with its fortifications, the Enneapylon, covered a far
wider area than is occupied by the Propylaea now; it took in the
whole West end of the hill and part of the North side, as well as
part of the South. The area included to the South was, as we
have already seen (p. 34), much larger than that to the North.

The Sanctuary of Zeus Olympios and the Pythion. The
two sanctuaries first mentioned, those of Zeus Olympios and of
Apollo Pythios, are linked together more closely than by mere

---

[1] *Class. Rev.* 1900, xiv. p. 279.

[2] Prof. Dörpfeld draws attention (*Rhein. Mus.* li. p. 134) to the analogous case
of Torone, which Thucydides (iv. 110) describes thus: οὔσης τῆς πόλεως πρὸς λόφον—
'was nach dem Zusammenhang nicht *nach dem Hügel hin* sondern nur *an dem
Hügel hinauf* bedeutet. But it must carefully be noted that as Dr Verrall (*Class.
Rev.* 1900, p. 278) observes, the notion of *ascent* is given not by πρὸς but by λόφον.
The analogy is one of fact, not of the verbal description of that fact.

topographical juxtaposition. In the Kerameikos Apollo Patroös[1]
had a temple close to the Stoa of Zeus Eleutherios; down near
the Ilissos, Zeus Olympios had his great sanctuary (Fig. 49),
and near it Apollo Pythios had a temenos, and here, where
Thucydides is speaking of the most ancient foundation of the
two gods, father and son, they are manifestly in close conjunction.
This is fortunate for our argument. For it happens that, whereas
we know the exact site of the earliest Pythion, of this earliest
Olympieion there are no certain remains. From the known site
of the Pythion and from the close conjunction of the two
we can deduce within narrow limits the unknown site of the
Olympion.

Possibly at this point, if the reader knows modern Athens, the
words 'the unknown site' of the Olympion will rouse an instinctive
protest. Surely the site of the Olympieion, with its familiar cluster
of Corinthian columns, is of all things most certain and familiar.
It lies South-East of the Acropolis not far from the Ilissos (see
Fig. 49). A moment's consideration will however show that this
Olympieion, though familiar, is irrelevant, nay impossible. It is
too remote to be described as *towards* the ancient city, it is too
recent to be accounted an ancient sanctuary. It was, as Thucydides
quite well knew, begun by Peisistratos[2].

We begin by fixing the site of the Pythion, happily certain.

Literature alone enables us within narrow limits to do this.
In the *Ion* of Euripides[3] Ion, learning that Creousa comes from
Athens, presses her for particulars about that 'glorious' city.
As a priestling he is naturally interested in all canonical legends,
but what he is really eager about is the ancient sacred spot which
linked Athens to Delphi. The nursling of Delphi eagerly asks

> And is there there a place called the Long Rocks?
> *Cre.* Why ask this? Oh the memory thou hast touched.
> *Ion.* The Pythian honours it and the Pythian fires.
> *Cre.* Honours it! he honours it! Curse the day I saw it.
> *Ion.* What is it? You hate the haunts the god loves best.
> *Cre.* Nothing. Those caves could tell a tale of shame.

But this is not what the pious Ion wants and he turns the
subject.

[1] Paus. I. 3. 4.
[2] For details of this Olympieion, see my *Myth. and. Mon. Anc. Athens*, p. 189.
[3] Eur. *Ion*, 283.

The place at Athens dearest to the Pythian, the place his lightnings honour is on the Long Rocks, and there, we may safely assume, was the god's earliest sanctuary.

The prologue of the same play tells us where the Long Rocks were, namely on the North of the Acropolis. Hermes, who brought Ion to Delphi, speaks[1]:

> 'A citadel there is in Hellas famed,
> Called after Pallas of the golden spear,
> And, where the northern rocks 'neath Pallas' hill
> Are called the Long Rocks, Phoebus there by force
> Did wed Creousa.'

Nor is it Ion only who knows that this place was honoured by the Pythian fires, it is no mere 'poetical' figure. Strabo[2], in speaking of a place called *Harma* in Boeotia, says we must not confuse this Harma with another Harma near Pyle, a deme in Attica bordering on Tanagra. In connection with this Attic Harma, he adds, the proverb originated 'When it has lightened through Harma.' Strabo further goes on to say that this Harma, which is on Mt Parnes, to the North-West of Athens, was watched by certain officials called Pythiasts for three days and nights in each of three successive months; when a flash of lightning was observed a sacrifice was despatched to Delphi. The place whence the observation was taken was the altar of Zeus Astrapaios, Zeus of the Lightning, and this altar was *in (or on) the (Acropolis) wall between the Pythion and the Olympion.*

Euripides, it is clear, is alluding to this definite ritual which of course would be familiar to Ion. That ritual he clearly conceived of as taking place near the Long Rocks. Near the Long Rocks must therefore have stood the altar of Zeus of the Lightning, on the wall between the Olympieion and the Pythion. Not only the Pythion but the Olympieion must therefore have been close to the Long Rocks. The word used by Strabo for *wall* ($\tau\epsilon\hat{\iota}\chi\sigma$) is strictly a fortification wall, and we should naturally understand it of that portion of the Pelargikon which defends the North-West corner of the citadel and abuts on the Long Rocks (Fig. 2). It is just here, close to the Pelargikon that we should, from the account of

---

[1] Eur. *Ion*, 7 ff.
[2] Strabo ix. 2 § 404 ἐτήρουν δ' ἐπὶ τρεῖς μῆνας, καθ' ἕκαστον μῆνα ἐπὶ τρεῖς ἡμέρας καὶ νύκτας ἀπὸ τῆς ἐσχάρας τοῦ Ἀστραπαίου Διός· ἔστι δ' αὕτη ἐν τῷ τείχει μεταξὺ τοῦ Πυθίου καὶ τοῦ Ὀλυμπίου.

Pausanias[1], expect to find Apollo's 'best loved' sanctuary.
Pausanias on leaving the Acropolis notes the Pelargikon, or as he
calls it Pelasgikon, and immediately after says 'on the descent not
to the lower parts of the city but just below the Propylaea, is a
spring of water, and close by a sanctuary of Apollo in a cave; they
think that it was here he met Creousa, the daughter of
Erechtheus.'

Pausanias says 'a sanctuary of Apollo in a cave.' It is the
fact that the sanctuary is in a cave that strikes and interests him.
He does not call it a *Pythion*. But by another writer the actual
word *Pythion* is used. Philostratos[2] describes the route taken by
the Panathenaic ship thus: starting from the outer Kerameikos it
sailed to the Eleusinion, and, having rounded it, it was carried
along past the Pelasgikon and came alongside of the Pythion,
where it is now moored. The Panathenaic way has been, as will
later be seen (p. 131), laid bare; for the moment all that concerns
us is that the Pythion is mentioned immediately after the
Pelasgikon and was therefore presumably next to it. Philostratos
puts what he calls the *Pythion* in just the place where Pausanias[3]
saw his 'sanctuary in a cave'; the two are identical. Further,
any doubts as to where the ship was moored are set at rest by
Pausanias himself. He saw the ship and noted its splendour.
It stood 'near the Areopagus.' The Pythion must have stood at
the North-West corner of the Acropolis (Fig. 46).

Even if we relied on literary evidence only we should be quite
sure that the Pythion of which Thucydides speaks was somewhere
on the Long Rocks, at the North-West end of the Acropolis.
Happily however the situation is not left thus vague; the actual
cave of Apollo has been found, and thoroughly cleared out, and
in it there came to light numerous inscribed votive offerings to
the god, which make the ascription certain.

From the lower tower at the North-West corner there have
always been clearly visible to any one looking up from below
three caves (Fig. 21), a very shallow one immediately over the

[1] Paus. I. 28. 4.
[2] Philostr. *Vit. Soph.* II. 5, p. 550 ἐκ Κεραμεικοῦ δὲ ἄρασαν χιλίᾳ κώπῃ ἀφεῖναι ἐπὶ
τὸ Ἐλευσίνιον καὶ περιβαλοῦσαν αὐτὸ παραμεῖψαι τὸ Πελασγικόν, κομιζομένην τε παρὰ τὸ
Πύθιον ἐλθεῖν οἳ νῦν ὥρμισται.
[3] Paus. I. 29. 1.

Klepsydra, and two others nearer together and somewhat deeper separated from the first by a shoulder of rock. On the plan in Fig. 22 these are marked A, B and Γ. The question has long been raised which of the three belonged to Apollo and which to Pan. As Pausanias[1] first mentions the sanctuary of Apollo in a cave and then passes on to tell the story of Pheidippides, manifestly *à propos*

Fig. 21.

of Pan's cave, it has been usual to connect A with Apollo and B and Γ, one or both, with Pan.

But the identification has never been felt to be quite satisfactory. The cave A is really no cave at all; it is a very shallow *niche*. It is impossible to imagine it the scene of the story of Creousa. Moreover it bears no traces of any votive offerings having been attached to its wall, nor have any remains of such been found there.

Between cave A and cave B there is a connecting stair-way *a, a′, a″*, but it should be carefully noted that A has no direct

[1] *loc. cit. supra.* Between the words νομίζουσι and ὡς πεμφθείη we must mentally supply ἐνταῦθα καὶ τοῦ Πανὸς ἱερόν, φασὶ δὲ, or words to that effect.

communication with the upper part of the Acropolis nor with

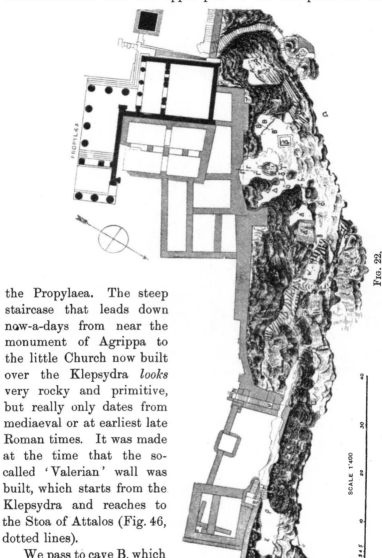

FIG. 22.

SCALE 1:400

the Propylaea. The steep
staircase that leads down
now-a-days from near the
monument of Agrippa to
the little Church now built
over the Klepsydra *looks*
very rocky and primitive,
but really only dates from
mediaeval or at earliest late
Roman times. It was made
at the time that the so-
called 'Valerian' wall was
built, which starts from the
Klepsydra and reaches to
the Stoa of Attalos (Fig. 46,
dotted lines).

We pass to cave B, which
formerly was believed to be-
long to Pan. Recent excavations[1] leave no doubt that it was

[1] The 'Valerian' wall was probably the work of Antonio Acciajoli. See
Dr Judeich, *Topographie von Athen*, p. 103, note 6.

sacred to Apollo. The back wall and sides of this cave are thickly
studded with *niches* for the most part of oblong shape, but a few
are round. About in the middle of the cave is an extra large
niche, which looks as if it had contained the image of a god.
Many of the *niches* still show the holes which once held nails
for the fixing of votive tablets. As the cave became unduly
crowded with offerings they overflowed on to the rock at the
left hand.

So far we are sure that cave B was a sanctuary, but of whom?
If A did not belong to Apollo we should expect that B, as next in
order, was Apollo's cave. The ground in front of B has been
cleared down to the living rock and the results of this clearance[1]
were conclusive. Exactly in front of B there came to light eleven
tablets or *pinakes* all of similar type, and all bearing inscribed
dedications to Apollo, either with the title 'below the Heights,'
or 'below the Long Rocks.' Cave B is clearly a sanctuary of
Apollo.

The votive tablets are all of late Roman date; it is probable
however that owing to the small space available, they superseded
earlier offerings of the same kind. The type scarcely varies.
Specimens are given in Fig. 23. The inscription is surrounded
sometimes by an olive wreath and sometimes by a myrtle wreath
with characteristic berries. Occasionally the wreath is tied by two
snakes. Two inscriptions may serve as a sample of the rest.
On No. 1[2] (Fig. 23) is inscribed 'Good Fortune G(aios) Ioulios
Metrodorus a Marathonian having borne the office of Thesmothetes
dedicated (this) to Apollo Below-the-Long (Rocks).' In the second[3]
instance (Fig. 23) the dedicator states that he is 'King' (Archon),
and the dedication is to Apollo 'below the Heights.' Clearly the
two titles of the god were interchangeable.

These dedications are of capital importance. It is little likely
that unless the custom had been of immemorial antiquity the

[1] For a full account of Dr Kabbadias's excavations from which the above
particulars are taken see *Ephemeris Archäologike,* 1897, 1—32 and 87—92, pl. I.—IV.
and for *résumé* in French *Bull. de Corr. Hell.* xx. 382 ff., also *American Journal of
Arch.* 1897, p. 348 and 1898, p. 311.

[2] 'Εφ. 'Αρχ. 1897, p. 8, pl. 4 'Αγαθὴ τύχη, Γ(άϊος) 'Ιούλιος Μητρόδωρος Μαραθ(ώνιος)
θεσμοθετήσας 'Απόλλωνι ὑπὸ Μακραῖς ἀνέθηκεν.

[3] 'Εφ. 'Αρχ. 1897, p. 9, pl. 4 Τιβ(έριος) 'Αντίστιος Κίνεας ἐκ Κοίλης 'Απόλλωνι ὑπ'
Ακραις βασιλεύς.

FIG. 23.

archons would have sought out an obscure cave-sanctuary in which to place their commemorative tablets. Was there not the temple of Apollo Patroös in the Market Place and the splendid Pythion down near the Ilissos?

They chose the cave-sanctuary of Apollo in which to place, at the close of their term of office, their votive tablet because it was in this ancient sanctuary that they had taken their oath of fidelity on their election. At the official scrutiny[1] of candidates for the archonship enquiry was made as to the ancestry of the candidate on both father's and mother's side. But it was not enough that he should be a full citizen, he was also solemnly asked whether he had an Apollo Patroös and a Zeus Herkeios and where their sanctuaries were. The Athenians, in so far as they were Ionians, claimed descent through Ion from Apollo and of course through Apollo from Zeus. The sanctuary in the cave was therefore to them of supreme importance. This scrutiny over, the candidates went to a sacred stone near the Stoa Basileios, and there, standing over the cut pieces of the sacrificed victim, they took the oath to rule justly and to take no bribes, and they swore that if any took a bribe he would dedicate at Delphi[2] a gold statue commensurate in value.

The archons had to prove their relation to Apollo Patroös and to dedicate a gold statue if they offended the Pythian god under whose immediate control they stood. Moreover it was not enough that they should swear at the Stoa Basileios. The oath was doubtless older than any Stoa Basileios in the later Market Place. After they had sworn there they had to 'go up to the Acropolis and there swear the same oath again[3].' Then and not till then could they enter office. And whither on the Acropolis should they go? Whither but to the cave where a little later they will dedicate their votive tablets, and where still the foundations of an altar stand, the cave of their ancestor Apollo Patroös and Pythios?

Whether the second oath, on the Acropolis, was taken actually

---

[1] Ar. 'Aθ. Πολ. LV. 15 and Harpocrat. *s.v.* 'Απόλλων Πατρῷος.

[2] Ar. 'Aθ. Πολ. LVII. 4. There is no mention of Delphi, and the word ἰσομέτρητον does not occur, but in Plato's reference (*Phaedr.* 235 D) it is distinctly stated both occur, καὶ σοι ἐγὼ ὥσπερ οἱ ἐννέα ἄρχοντες, ὑπισχνοῦμαι χρυσῆν εἰκόνα ἰσομέτρητον εἰς Δελφοὺς ἀναθήσειν.

[3] Ar. 'Aθ. Πολ. LV. 5 ἐντεῦθεν δ' ὀμόσαντες εἰς ἀκρόπολιν βαδίζουσιν καὶ πάλιν ἐκεῖ ταῦτα ὀμνύουσι.

in the cave-sanctuary cannot be certainly decided; the votive tablets make it probable and they make quite certain that the cave-sanctuary was officially used by the archons. This fact it is necessary to emphasize. Until these inscriptions were brought to light Apollo's cave was thought to be of but little importance, curious and primitive but practically negligible. Now that it is clear that the archons selected it as their memorial chapel, such a view is no longer possible. It was a sanctuary not merely of Apollo Below-the-Heights but of the ancestral god, the Apollo Patroös of the archons. Moreover—a fact all important—this Apollo 'Below-the-Heights' being Apollo Patroös was also Apollo Pythios. Demosthenes in the *de Corona*[1], calling to witness his country's gods, says ' I call on all the gods and goddesses who hold the land of Attica and on Apollo the Pythian, who is ancestral ($\pi\alpha\tau\rho\hat{\omega}\text{os}$) to the state.' The sanctuary in the cave was a Python. Apollo coming as he did to Athens from Pytho was always Pythian whatever additional title he might take, and every sanctuary of his was a Python; his most venerable sanctuary was not a temple but a hollowed rock.

The Python lies before us securely fixed, primitive, convincing. With the 'sanctuary of Zeus Olympios' it is alas! far otherwise. Given that the Python is fixed at the North-West corner of the Acropolis, and given that, according to Strabo (see p. 69), it was so near the Olympieion that the place of an altar could be described as 'between' them, then it follows that somewhere near to that North-West corner the sanctuary of Zeus Olympios must have lain. We may further say that as Thucydides, it will be seen, notes the various sanctuaries and the city-well in the order from East to West, and begins with the sanctuary of Zeus Olympios, it lay presumably somewhat to the East of the Python. To the East of the Python, near to the supposed site of the temenos of Aglauros, was found an inscription[2] with a dedication to Zeus, but, as inscriptions are easily moveable, no great importance can be attached to this isolated fact. Of definite monumental evidence for the existence of a sanctuary of Zeus where we seek it,

---

[1] Dem. *de Cor.* 275 καλῶ...καὶ τὸν Ἀπόλλω τὸν Πύθιον ὃς πατρῷός ἐστι τῇ πόλει.
[2] *C.I.A.* III. 198.

we must frankly own at the outset there is nothing certain[1]. It must stand or fall with the Pythion.

Before examining such literary evidence as exists it is necessary to note clearly that Thucydides mentions not a *temple* but a *sanctuary*. The great temple near the Ilissos, begun by Peisistratos[2], and not completed till centuries later by Antiochus Epiphanes and Hadrian, is usually spoken of as a temple (*ναός*), but we have no grounds whatever for supposing that on or near the Long Rocks there was a temple, but only a sanctuary[3], which may very likely have been merely a precinct with an altar. Such a precinct and altar might easily disappear and leave no trace. This is of importance for the understanding of what follows.

When we come to literary evidence one point is clear. Before Peisistratos began the building of his great *temple* there existed another and earlier place for the worship of Zeus, and this is spoken of as not a temple but a sanctuary. Pausanias[4], when he visited the great temple, wrote, 'They say that Deucalion built the old sanctuary of Zeus Olympios, and, as a proof of the sojourn of Deucalion at Athens, point to his tomb, which is not far distant from the present temple.'

It has usually been assumed that this earlier sanctuary was on or near the site of the later temple, but, as Prof. Dörpfeld[5] has pointed out, this is no-wise stated by Pausanias. He only says that there was a *tomb* of Deucalion, not far from the present temple, and that the existence of this tomb made people attribute to Deucalion the building of the early sanctuary. Where the early sanctuary was he does *not* say. It should be noted that he is careful to use the word *sanctuary*, not temple, in speaking of the foundation of Deucalion.

---

[1] Prof. Dörpfeld kindly tells me that he thinks it quite possible that the poros structure below and north of the Klepsydra may be remains of the Olympion. The situation would of course admirably suit the words of Thucydides. The remains are marked in solid black in Fig. 46.

[2] For full particulars of this temple see my *Myth. and Mon. Anc. Athens*, p. 190.

[3] I see to my great regret that Prof. Ernest Gardner in translating Thucydides II. 15 renders ἱερόν throughout by '*temple*,' 'the temple of Olympian Zeus, the Pythium, the temple of Earth.' Though *templum* in Latin is used to denote any sanctified space of earth or air, surely such a use of *temple* is misleading in English.

[4] Paus. I. 18. 9 τοῦ δὲ Ὀλυμπίου Διὸς Δευκαλίωνα οἰκοδομῆσαι λέγουσι τὸ ἀρχαῖον ἱερὸν σημεῖον ἀποφαίνοντες ὡς Δευκαλίων Ἀθήνῃσιν ᾤκησε τάφον τοῦ ναοῦ τοῦ νῦν οὐ πολὺ ἀφεστηκότα.

[5] *A. Mitt.* 1895, p. 56. The word οἰκοδομέω does not necessarily imply house or temple building. It is used of building a wall, a labyrinth.

From this it follows, I think, that when we hear of a *sanctuary* of Zeus Olympios, not a temple, there is a slight presumption in favour of its being the earlier foundation. In the opening scene of the *Phaedrus*[1] an 'Olympion,' i.e. a sanctuary of Zeus, is mentioned. Socrates and Phaedrus meet somewhere, presumably within the city walls, for Socrates is later taxed with never going for a country walk. Socrates says, 'So it seems Lysias was up in town.' Phaedrus answers, 'Yes, he is staying with Epikrates in yonder house, near the Olympion, the one that used to belong to Morychus.' The favourite haunt of Socrates was the agora; a stroll by the Ilissos was to him a serious and unusual country walk. Our Olympion at the North-West corner of the Acropolis would fit the scene somewhat better than the great temple near the Ilissos; but that is all, the passage *proves* nothing.

A question more important perhaps than any topographical issue remains. Do we know anything of the nature of the god worshipped in the ancient sanctuary, or of the character of his ritual? The question may seem to some superfluous. Zeus is surely Zeus everywhere and for all time, his cloud-compelling nature and his splendid sacrificial feasts familiar from Homer downwards. But then what of Deucalion? Deucalion is a figure manifestly Oriental, a feeble copy of the archetypal Noah. Why does he institute the worship of our immemorial Indo-European Zeus? Are there two Zeuses?

There were, at least at Athens, two festivals of Zeus. Thucydides[2] himself is witness. He tells us of the trap laid for Kylon in characteristic fashion by the Delphic oracle. Kylon was to seize the Acropolis 'on the greatest festival of Zeus.' But this 'greatest festival' was alas for him! not of the Zeus he, as an Olympian victor, remembered, but of 'Zeus Meilichios,' and—significant fact for us—it, the familiar Diasia, was celebrated 'outside the city.' This 'outside the city' cannot fail, used as the words are by Thucydides himself, to remind us of our sanctuary, also 'outside.'

---

[1] Plat. *Phaedr.* 227 Σω. ἀτὰρ Λυσίας ἦν ὡς ἔοικεν ἐν ἄστει; Φαι. Ναὶ παρ᾽ Ἐπικράτει ἐν τῇδε τῇ πλησίον τοῦ Ὀλυμπίου οἰκίᾳ τῇ Μορυχίᾳ. Nothing can be inferred from ἐν ἄστει. It means simply 'in town' as opposed to the Peiraeus or the country.

[2] Thucyd. I. 126 ἔστι γὰρ καὶ Ἀθηναίοις Διάσια ἃ καλεῖται Διὸς ἑορτὴ Μειλιχίου μεγίστη, ἔξω τῆς πόλεως.

What may be dimly discerned, though certainly no-wise demonstrated, is this. The name *Zeus* is one of the few divine titles as to which philologists agree that it is Indo-European. But the name Zeus was attached to persons and conceptions many and diverse, and here in Athens it was attached to a divinity of Oriental nature and origin. Meilichios[1] is but the Graecized form of Melek, the 'King' best known to us as Moloch, a deity who like the Greek Meilichios loved holocausts, a deity harsh and stern, who could only by a helpless and hopelessly mistaken etymology be called Meilichios the Gentle One. His worship prevailed in the Peiraeus, brought thither probably by Phenician sailors, from his sanctuary there came the familiar reliefs with the great snake as the impersonation of the god. It was this Semitic Melek whom Deucalion brought in his ark. When this Semitic immigration took place it is hard to say. Tradition, as evidenced by the *Parian Chronicle*[2], placed it in the reign of the shadowy Attic king Kranaos, about 1528 B.C.

The sanctuaries of both Zeus and Apollo are alike outside the ancient city. Zeus had altars on the Acropolis itself; Apollo, great though he was, never forced an entrance there. The fact is surely significant. Herodotus[3], it will be remembered, marks the successive stages of the development of Athens: under Kekrops they were Kekropidai, under Erechtheus they were Athenians, and last, 'when Ion, son of Xuthos, became their leader, from him they were called Ionians.' Ion was the first Athenian polemarch[4].

One thing is clear, Ion marks the incoming of a new race, a race with Zeus and Apollo for their gods. From the blend of this new stock with the old autochthonous inhabitants arose the

---

[1] For a discussion of the worship of Meilichios see my *Prolegomena*, pp. 12—29. What I there say as to the chthonic character of Meilichios still I hope holds good, but I offer my apologies to M. Foucart for my attempted refutation of his theory as to the Semitic origin of the god. I now see that he was right. Meilichios is none other than מֶ֫לֶךְ misunderstood. See also Lagrange, *Études sur les Religions Sémitiques*, 1905, pp. 99—109.

[2] *Par. Chron.* (Jacobi) 6 Βασιλεύοντος Ἀθηνῶν Κρ[ανα]οῦ ἀφ' οὗ κατακλυσμὸς ἐπὶ Δευκαλίωνος ἐγένετο καὶ Δευκαλίων τοὺς ὄμβρους ἔφυγεν ἐγ Λυκωρείας εἰς Ἀθήνας πρὸ[s Κρανα]ὸν καὶ τοῦ Διὸ[s το]ῦ Ὀ[λυ]μ[πί]ου τὸ ἱ[ε]ρὸν ἱδ[ρύσατ]ο [καὶ] τὰ σωτήρια ἔθυσεν. I would suggest that behind Kranaos hides another Semitic figure, Kronos.

[3] Herod. VIII. 44.

[4] Schol. ad Ar. *Av.* 1527 πατρῷον δὲ τιμῶσιν Ἀπόλλωνα Ἀθηναῖοι, ἐπεὶ Ἴων ὁ πολέμαρχος Ἀθηναίων ἐξ Ἀπόλλωνος καὶ Κρεούσης τῆς Ξούθου ἐγένετο.

Ionians. Zeus and Apollo were called 'ancestral' at Athens because they *were* ancestral; the new element traced its descent from them, and presumably the affiliation was arranged by Delphi; but Apollo, though his sanctuary was *on* the hill, never got *in*side.

Ion had for divine father Apollo, but his real human father was Xuthos. This Xuthos, as immigrant conqueror, marries the king's daughter Creousa. Xuthos was really a local hero of the deme Potamoi[1], near Prasiae. He came of Achaean stock, and therefore had Zeus for ancestor. Hermes, in the prologue to the *Ion*[2], is quite clear. There was war between Athens and Euboea:

> And Xuthos strove and helped them with the sword
> And had Creousa, guerdon of his aid,
> No home-born hero he, but son of Zeus
> And Aiolos, Achaean.

And again[3], when Ion questions his unknown mother as to her husband:

> *Ion.* And what Athenian took thee for his wife?
> *Cre.* No citizen: an alien from another land.
> *Ion.* Who? For a well-born man he needs had been.
> *Cre.* Xuthos, of Zeus and Aiolos the offspring he.

The tomb of Ion, significant fact, was not at Athens but at Potamoi, and Pausanias[4] saw it there. Well may the sanctuaries of Zeus and Apollo stand together.

To return to the question of topography. That the cave marked B on the plan is sacred to Apollo admits, in the face of the inscribed votive tablets, of no doubt. But a difficulty yet remains. It was noted in speaking of the cave above the Klepsydra that it was too shallow and too exposed to be a natural scene of the story of Creousa. The same objections, though in a somewhat less degree, apply to the cave marked B. The difficulty, however, admits of an easy solution.

The excavators proceeded to clear out cave Γ, and here they found nothing, no votive tablets, no altar, no inscriptions. But in carrying on their work further East they came on a fourth cave, of a character quite different from that of A, B, or Γ. The fourth

---

[1] Paus. i. 31. 2.   [2] Eur. *Ion*, 57—64.   [3] Eur. *Ion*, 289—295.
[4] Paus. vii. 1. 2, and see *Myth. and Mon. Anc. Athens*, p. lxxxi.

cave, Δ, has a very narrow entrance; it communicates by a narrow passage with Δ' and also with Δ", but Δ" has been turned into a small Christian church, of which the pavement and a portion of a brick wall yet remain. Here at Δ we have a cave in the full sense of the word, and here we have in all probability the cave or caves, the 'seats[1]' (θακήματα) of Pan.

But, be it remembered, Pan was a late comer; his worship was introduced after his services at Marathon. In heroic days, the time of the story of Creousa, the Long Rocks were shared by the Pythian god and the daughters of Aglauros. The hollow triple cave marked Δ', Δ", Δ''' was once the property of Apollo, and it saw the birth of Ion; later it was handed over to Pan, and is again, as in the *Lysistrata*[2], the natural sequestered haunt of lovers. Kinesias, on the Acropolis, points out to Myrrhine that near at hand is the sanctuary of Pan for seclusion, and close by the Klepsydra for purification.

In the countless votive tablets[3] to Pan and. the nymphs, the type varies little. We have a cave, an altar: round the altar three nymphs are dancing, usually led by Hermes, and, perched on the side of the cave or looking through a hole, Pan is piping to them. The three nymphs, three daughters of Kekrops, were then dancing on the Long Rocks long before Pan came to pipe to them. Concerned as we are for the present with Apollo and his Pythion, it is only necessary to note that their shrine, the sanctuary of Aglauros, must have been near the cave of Pan, somewhere to the East. Euripides[4] speaks of them as practically one:

> O seats of Pan and rock hard by
> To where the hollow Long Rocks lie
> Where, before Pallas' temple-bound
> Aglauros' daughters three go round
> Upon their grassy dancing-ground
> To nimble reedy staves.
> Where thou O Pan art piping found
> Within thy shepherd caves.

Exactly where that sanctuary of Aglauros was excavations have not established. At the point where the cavern is closed by the little modern church, begins a stairway, consisting of seventeen steps (θ-κ-λ-μ-), cut in the rock. These steps manifestly lead up to the

---

[1] Eur. *Ion*, 492.   [2] Ar. *Lys.* 911.
[3] See *Myth. and Mon. Anc. Athens*, p. 546.
[4] Eur. *Ion*, 492, trans. Mr D. S. MacColl.

steps already known, which lead down, twenty-two in number, from the Erechtheion. This is probably the 'opening' (ὄπη) down which the deserting women in the *Lysistrata*[1] were caught escaping. Still further East is a long narrow subterranean passage, a natural cleft in the rock π—π′, and at the end of this, just above the modern Church of the Seraphim, is supposed to be the sanctuary of Aglauros. Here were found a niche in the rock, the basis of a statue, and some fragments of black-figured vases. Here again there is communication with the Acropolis, but only by a ladder ascending the cliff for about twenty feet at a precipitous point. Moreover the upper part of the stone stairway is of mediaeval date so that it is not likely that the ascent was an ancient one.

The Sanctuary of Ge.—The site of this sanctuary can, within very narrow limits be determined.

Pausanias, in describing the South side of the Acropolis, after passing the Asklepieion, notes the temple of Themis and the monument of Hippolytus. Apropos of this he mentions and probably saw a sanctuary of Aphrodite Pandemos (p. 105); he then says 'there is also a sanctuary of Ge Kourotrophos and Demeter Chloe'; immediately afterwards he passes through the Propylaea. The sanctuary of Ge must therefore have been at the South-West corner or due West of the Acropolis, and presumably somewhere along the winding road followed by Pausanias (see Plan, p. 38). From the account of Pausanias[2] we should gather that Ge Kourotrophos, Earth the Nursing-Mother, and Demeter Chloe, Green Demeter had a sanctuary together; perhaps they had by the time of Pausanias, but the considerable number of separate dedications[3] to Demeter Chloe makes it probable that at least in earlier days these precincts, though near, were distinct.

The union of Ge Kourotrophos and Demeter Chloe is not the union of Mother and Maid, it is the union of two Mother-goddesses. Of the two Demeter belongs locally not to Athens but to Eleusis. Ge Kourotrophos is obviously the earlier and strictly local figure. But Demeter of Eleusis, from various

---

[1] Ar. *Lys.* 720 τὴν μὲν δὲ πρώτην διαλέγουσαν τὴν ὄπιν.
[2] Paus. I. 22. 3.
[3] For a full list of these see Dr Frazer on P. I. 22. 3.

causes, political and agricultural, developed to dimensions almost Olympian, and her figure tended everywhere to efface that of the local Earth-Mother, hence we need not be surprised that the number of dedications to Demeter is larger than that of those to Kourotrophos. Kourotrophos appears among the early divinities enumerated by the woman herald in the *Thesmophoriazusae*[1], and the scholiast, in his comment on the passage, recognizes her antiquity : ' either Earth or Hestia ; it comes to the same thing ; they sacrifice to her before Zeus.' Suidas[2] states that Erichthonios was the first to sacrifice to her on the Acropolis, and instituted the custom that ' those who were sacrificing to any god should first sacrifice to her.'

The Sanctuary of Dionysos-in-the-Marshes.

The name Dionysos at once carries us in imagination to the famous theatre on the South side of the Acropolis (Fig. 16), and we remember perhaps with some relief that this theatre is, quite as much as the Pythion, 'towards' the ancient city; it lies right up against the Acropolis rock. We remember also that Pausanias[3], in his account of the South slope, says ' the oldest sanctuary of Dionysos is beside the theatre.' He sees within the precinct there two temples, the foundations of which remain to-day ; one of them was named Eleutherian, the other we think may surely have belonged to Dionysos-in-the-Marshes. It is true that the ground about the theatre is anything but marshy now, nor could it ever have been very damp, as it slopes sharply down to the South-East. Still, from an ancient name it is never safe to argue[4]; *in-the-marshes may* have been a mere popular etymology from a word the meaning of which was wholly lost.

But a moment's reflection shows that the identification, though tempting, will not do. Thucydides himself (p. 66) seems to warn us;

[1] Ar. *Thesm.* 300 καὶ τῇ Κουροτρόφῳ τῇ Γῇ, schol. εἴτε τῇ γῇ εἴτε τῇ ἑστίᾳ, ὁμοίως πρὸ τοῦ Διὸς θύουσιν αὐτῇ.

[2] Suidas, *s.v.* Κουροτρόφος Γῆ...καταστῆσαι δὲ νόμιμον τοὺς θύοντάς τινι θεῷ ταύτῃ προθύειν.

[3] Paus. I. 20. 3. See Mr Mitchell Carroll in the *Classical Review* (July 1905, p. 325), 'Thucydides, Pausanias and the Dionysium in Limnis,' but Mr Carroll makes the to my mind fatal mistake of examining the Limnae question apart from the other sanctuaries.

[4] See Dr Verrall (*Class. Rev.* xiv. 1900, p. 278), who cites Burnham Beeches which has nothing to do with any *beech* and Sandiacre which has nothing to do with *sand*, and, as Mr Carroll observes, 'Rhode Island' is not an island nor is Washington a Washing-Town.

he seems to say, 'not that precinct which you all know so well and think so much of, not that theatre where year by year you all go, but an earlier and more venerable place, and, that there be no mistake, the place where you go on the 12th day of Anthesterion, and where your ancestors went before they migrated to colonize Asia Minor.'

It is most fortunate that Thucydides has been thus precise, because about this festival on the 12th day of Anthesterion we know from other sources[1] certain important details which may help to the identification of the sanctuary.

The festival celebrated on the 12th of Anthesterion was the Festival of the Choes or Pitchers[2]. On this day, we learn from Athenaeus[3] and others, the people drank new wine, each one by himself, offered some to the god, and brought to the priestess in the sanctuary in the Marshes the wreaths they had worn. On this day took place also a ceremony of great sanctity, the marriage of the god to the wife of the chief archon—the 'king' as he was called. The actual marriage took place in a building called the Boukoleion, the exact site of which is not known; but certain preliminary ceremonies were gone through by the Bride in the sanctuary in-the-Marshes. The author of the Oration ' *against Neaera*[4]' tells us that there was a law by which the Bride had to be a full citizen and a virgin when she married the king, she was bound over to perform the ceremonies required of her ' according to ancestral custom,' to leave nothing undone, and to introduce no innovations. This law, the orator tells us, was engraved on a stele and set up alongside of the altar in the sanctuary of Dionysos in-the-Marshes, and remained to his day, though the letters were somewhat dim.

But this, though much, is not all. The orator goes on to tell us why the law was written up in this particular sanctuary. 'And

---

[1] Such sources as are necessary for my argument will be given as required, but the whole material for the study of the Attic festivals of Dionysos has been collected by Dr Martin P. N. Nilsson in his *Studia de Dionysiis Atticis*, Lund, 1900.

[2] For the ceremonies see my *Prolegomena*, p. 40.

[3] Athen. XI. p. 464 F. Φανόδημος δὲ πρὸς τῷ ἱερῷ φησὶ τοῦ ἐν Λίμναις Διονύσου τὸ γλεῦκος φέροντας τοὺς Ἀθηναίους ἐκ τῶν πίθων τῷ θεῷ κιρνάναι: and X. 437 B...ἀποφέρειν τοὺς στεφάνους πρὸς τὸ ἐν Λίμναις τέμενος.

[4] [Dem.] c. *Neaer.* § 73 καὶ τοῦτον τὸν νόμον γράψαντες ἐν στήλῃ λιθίνῃ ἔστησαν ἐν τῷ ἱερῷ τοῦ Διονύσου παρὰ τὸν βωμὸν ἐν Λίμναις.

III] *Sanctuary of Dionysos-in-the-Marshes* 85

the reason why they set it up in the most ancient sanctuary of Dionysos and the most holy, in the Marshes, is that not many people may read what is written. For it is opened once only in each year, on the 12th of the month Anthesterion[1].' Finally, having sufficiently raised our curiosity, he bids the clerk read the actual oath administered by this pure Bride to her attendants, administered before they touch the sacred things, and taken *on* the baskets at the altar. The clerk is to read it that all present may realize how venerable and holy and ancient the accustomed rite was. The oath of the attendants was as follows: ' *I fast and am clean and abstinent from all things that make unclean and from intercourse with man, and I will celebrate the Theoïnia and the Iobakcheia to Dionysos in accordance with ancestral usage and at the appointed times.*'

We shall meet again the precinct, the altar, the stele, the oath; for the present it is all-important to note that the precinct *In-the-Marshes* was open but once a year, and that on the 12th of Anthesterion. It is impossible, therefore, that this precinct could be identical with the precinct near the theatre on the South slope[2], as this must have been open for the Greater Dionysia, celebrated in the month Elaphebolion (March—April).

The precinct *In-the-Marshes* has been sought and found; but before we tell the story of its finding, in order that we may realize what clue was in the hands of the excavators, it is necessary to say a word as to the time and place of the festivals of Dionysos at Athens.

Thucydides himself tells us that the Dionysiac festivals were two, an earlier and a later. His use of the comparative—'Dionysos-in-the-Marshes,' he says, ' to whom is celebrated the *more ancient* Dionysiac Festival,'—makes it clear that, to his mind, there were two and only two. The later festival, the Greater Dionysia, was celebrated in the precinct of Dionysos Eleuthereus; the time, we noted before, was the month Elaphebolion.

---

[1] *c. Neaer.* § 76 καὶ διὰ ταῦτα ἐν τῷ ἀρχαιοτάτῳ ἱερῷ τοῦ Διονύσου καὶ ἁγιωτάτῳ ἐν Λίμναις ἔστησαν ἵνα μὴ πολλοὶ εἰδῶσι τὰ γεγραμμένα· ἅπαξ γὰρ τοῦ ἐνιαυτοῦ ἐκάστου ἀνοίγεται, τῇ δωδεκάτῃ τοῦ Ἀνθεστηριῶνος μηνός.

[2] This and the separate character of the festivals belonging to the Limnae from those of the precinct of Dionysos Eleuthereus were first pointed out I believe by Professor W. v. Wilamowitz-Moellendorff, 'Die Bühne von Æschylos,' *Hermes* XXI. p. 617.

The 'more ancient Dionysiac Festival' is of course a purely informal descriptive title. But it happens that we know the official title of the two Athenian festivals, the earlier and the later[1].

1. The later festival, that in the present theatre, was called in laws and official inscriptions ' the (Dionysia) in the town (τὰ ἐν ἄστει), or ' the town Dionysia' (ἀστικὰ Διονύσια).

2. The more ancient festival was called either ' the Dionysia at the Lenaion' (τὰ ἐπὶ Ληναίῳ Διονύσια), or 'the (dramatic) contest at the Lenaion' (ὁ ἐπὶ Ληναίῳ ἀγών), or, more simply, 'the Lenaia' (τὰ Λήναια).

We have got two *festivals*, an earlier and a later, the earlier called officially 'Lenaia,' or 'the dramatic contest at the Lenaion'; but were there two *theatres* also, an earlier and a later? Yes. Pollux[2] tells us there was a Dionysiac theatre and a 'Lenaic' one — just the very word we wanted. And to clinch the whole argument we find that the 'Lenaic' one was the earlier. Hesychius[3], explaining the phrase, 'the dramatic contest at the Lenaion,' says, ' there is in the city the Lenaion with a large enclosure, and in it a sanctuary of Dionysos Lenaios. In this (*i.e.* presumably the enclosure) the dramatic contests of the Athenians took place, before the theatre was built.'

This 'theatre,' where the plays were performed before the theatre of Eleuthereus was built, was no very grand affair; its seats, it would seem, were called 'scaffoldings' (ἴκρια). Photius[4] in explaining the word *ikria* says, ' the (structure) in the agora from which they watched the Dionysiac contests before the theatre in the precinct of Dionysos was built.'

Photius, while explaining the 'scaffolding,' gives us incidentally a priceless piece of information. This early theatre was *in the agora.*

---

[1] The sources are (1) the law of Euegoros (Dem. *c. Meid.* 10) Εὐήγορος εἶπεν· ὅταν ἡ πομπὴ ᾖ τῷ Διονύσῳ ἐν Πειραιεῖ καὶ οἱ κωμῳδοὶ καὶ οἱ τραγῳδοί, καὶ ἡ ἐπὶ Ληναίῳ πομπὴ καὶ οἱ τραγῳδοὶ καὶ οἱ κωμῳδοί, καὶ τοῖς ἐν ἄστει Διονυσίοις ἡ πομπή...; (2) an official inscription, *C.I.A.* II. 741, in which the same two festivals are three times mentioned.

[2] Poll. *On.* IV. 121 καὶ Διονυσιακὸν θέατρον καὶ Ληναϊκόν.

[3] Hesych. *s.v.* ἐπὶ Ληναίῳ ἀγών· ἔστιν ἐν τῷ ἄστει Λήναιον περίβολον ἔχον μέγαν, καὶ ἐν αὐτῷ Ληναίου Διονύσου ἱερόν, ἐν ᾧ ἐπετελοῦντο οἱ ἀγῶνες Ἀθηναίων πρὶν τὸ θέατρον οἰκοδομηθῆναι. The same account is given by Photius *s.v.* Λήναιον, by the *Etym. Magnum* ἐπὶ Ληναίῳ and Bekker's *Anecdota* I. p. 278.

[4] Phot. *s.v.* ἴκρια· τὰ ἐν τῇ ἀγορᾷ, ἀφ' ὧν ἐθεῶντο τοὺς Διονυσιακοὺς ἀγῶνας πρὶν ἢ κατασκευασθῆναι τὸ ἐν Διονύσου θέατρον, and see also Eustath. 1472, 7, and Hesych. *s.v.* παρ' αἰγείρον θέα. Hesychius quotes Eratosthenes from whom very probably all the other accounts came.

But then, to raise a time-honoured question, to which we shall later (p. 132) return, where is the agora ? This question for the present we must not pursue. But the ancient theatre consisted of more than 'scaffolding' for seats. It had what was the central, initial, cardinal feature of every Greek theatre, its dancing place, its *orchestra*; and we know approximately where this orchestra was. A lexicographer[1], explaining the word *orchestra*, says, ' a conspicuous place for a public festival, where are the statues of Harmodios and Aristogeiton.'

The agora, conducted by successive theorists, has made the complete tour of the Acropolis, but the statues of the Tyrant-Slayers cannot break loose from the Areopagus,—beneath which 'not far' from the temple of Ares, Pausanias[2] saw them. The statues, according to Timaeus, were at the site of the ancient orchestra[3], from the scaffolding of which 'in the agora' the more ancient festival (the Lenaia) was witnessed. Here then, somewhere near the Areopagus, we must seek the sanctuary of Dionysos-in-the-Marshes.

The Lenaia, though more ancient than the 'city Dionysia,' was no obscure festival. Plato[4], in the *Protagoras*, mentions a comedy which Pherecrates had brought out at the Lenaia, and it can never be forgotten that for the Lenaia, in 405 B.C., Aristophanes wrote the *Frogs*[5]. The chorus of Frogs[6] assuredly remember that their home is in the Limnae. There they were

---

[1] Tim. *Lex. Plat.* 'Ορχήστρα τόπος ἐπιφάνης εἰς πανήγυριν ἔνθα 'Αρμοδίου καὶ 'Αριστογείτονος εἰκόνες.

[2] Paus. I. 8. 4.

[3] To any one using my *Mythology and Monuments of Ancient Athens* I must at this point offer my apologies. The rough sketch map of the agora (facing p. 5) was made before Prof. Dörpfeld's excavations. The *Limnae* is wrongly marked on the district near the Dipylon. I was at that time convinced only that the *Limnae* did *not* lie South of the Acropolis and wrongly identified it with the sanctuary seen by Pausanias on his entrance into the city. The *orchestra* also on my plan must be moved further to the South-East. The conjectural site of the Odeion seen by Pausanias is shown on Prof. Dörpfeld's plan (Fig. 46). At this point a curved foundation of Roman masonry has come to light.

[4] Plat. *Prot.* 327.

[5] Ar. *Ran. Hyp.* ἐδιδάχθη ἐπὶ Καλλίου τοῦ μετὰ 'Αντιγένη διὰ Φιλωνίδου εἰς Λήναια.

[6] Ar. *Ran.* 218

> ἦν ἀμφὶ Νυσήιον
> Διὸς Διόνυσον ἐν
> Λήμναις ἰαχήσαμεν
> ἡνίχ' ὁ κραιπαλόκωμος
> τοῖς ἱεροῖσι Χύτροισι
> χωρεῖ κατ' ἐμὸν τέμενος λαῶν ὄχλος.

Trans. by Mr Gilbert Murray. For the χύτρινοι ἀγῶνες, see Schol. *ad loc.*, ἤγοντο ἀγῶνες αὐτόθι οἱ χύτρινοι καλούμενοι καθ' ἅ φησιν Φιλόχορος ἐν τῇ ἐκτῇ τῶν 'Ατθίδων.

wont to croak and chant at the Anthesteria, on the third day of which festival, the Chytroi or Pots, came the 'Pot Contests,' probably the earliest dramatic performances that Athens saw.

'O brood of the mere, the spring,
Gather together and sing
   From the depths of your throat
   By the side of the boat
Co-äx, as we move in a ring;

As in Limnae we sang the divine
Nyseïan Giver of Wine,
   When the people in lots
   With their sanctified Pots
Came reeling around my shrine.'

The excavations which have brought to light the ancient sanctuary of the Limnae were not undertaken solely, or even chiefly, with that object.   Rather the intention was to settle, if possible, other and wider topographical questions: where lay the ancient road to the Acropolis, where the ancient agora, and where the city well, Kallirrhoë.   Yet, to some, who awaited with an almost breathless impatience the result of these excavations, their great hope was that the precinct of the Limnae might be found; that they might know where in imagination to picture the ancient rites of the Anthesteria and the marriage of the Queen and those earliest dramatic contests from which sprang tragedy and comedy.   The wider results of the excavations will be noted in connection with the Enneakrounos; for the moment it is the narrower, intenser issue of the *Limnae* that alone concerns us.

So far our only topographical clues have been two.   (1) Thucydides has told us that the sanctuary in the Marshes with the other sanctuaries he mentions was '*towards*' the ancient city; we have fixed the Pythion at the North-West corner of the Acropolis, and as his account seems to be moving westwards, we expect the Dionysiac sanctuary to be West of that point.   (2) We know also (p. 87) that the ancient orchestra was near the Areopagus. We look for a site for the Dionysia which shall combine these two directions.   If that site is also a possible Marsh, so much the better; and here indeed, in the hollow between the Pnyx, Areopagus, and Acropolis, water is caught and confined; but for artificial drainage, here marsh-land must be.   This, by practical experience, the excavators soon had reason to know.

A portion of the results of the excavations begun by the German Archaeological Institute in 1887[1] and lasting for upwards

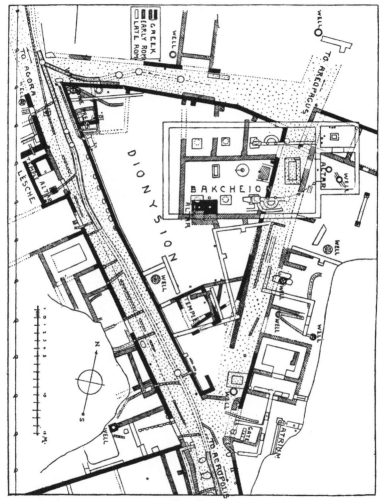

FIG. 24.

of ten years is to be seen on the plans in Figs. 24 and 35). The enlarged plan of a portion of the excavations (Fig. 24) for

[1] For the literature of the excavations see Bibliography. A *résumé* of the portion relating to the *Limnae* will be found in Dr Frazer's *Pausanias*, vol. v. p. 495, Addenda, Athens.

the moment alone concerns us. The first substantial discovery that rewarded the excavators was the finding of the ancient road. It followed, as Professor Dörpfeld had always predicted it would, the lie of the modern road. Roads being strictly conditioned by the law of least resistance do not lightly alter their course. The present carriage road to the Acropolis is a little less devious in its windings than the ancient one, that is all (Fig. 35).

Just below where the ancient road passes down from the West shoulder of the Acropolis, and at a level much higher than that of the road itself, the excavators came on a building of Roman date and indifferent masonry, which proved to be a large hall, with two rows of columns dividing it into a central nave and two aisles. To the East the hall was furnished with a quadrangular apse. Within this apse was found an altar[1] decorated with scenes from the worship of Dionysos, a goat being dragged to the altar, a Satyr, a Maenad, and the like. This altar would in itself rouse the suspicion that we are in a sanctuary dedicated to Dionysos, but fortunately we are not left to evidence so precarious.

Of far greater interest than the altar, and indeed for our purpose of supreme importance, was another

Inscription Athen. Mitth.. XIX. 1894. p 249.

FIG. 25.

<hr />

[1] H. Schrader, 'Funde im Bezirk des Dionysion,' *A. Mitt.* 1896, xxi. p. 265, pl. ix.

discovery. In the apse, with the altar mentioned and other altars, was found the drum of a column (Fig. 25), which had once stood in the great hall ; columns just like it are still standing, so that it belongs without doubt to the building. On it is an inscription[1], divided into two columns and 167 lines in length, which from its style may be dated about the third century A.D. Above the inscription, in a relief in pediment form containing Dionysiac symbols, two panthers stand heraldically, one to either side of a *cantharus*; above is the head of a bull. Inscriptions arranged in this fashion on columns are not unusual in the third century A.D.[2]

The inscription contains the statutes of a *thiasos*, or club of persons calling themselves Iobakchoi, who met in a place—the hall where the inscription was set up—called the Bakcheion. This is our quadrangular building marked *Bakcheion* on the plan (Fig. 24). The rules, which are given in great detail, are very interesting, but for the present one thing only concerns us—the name of the thiasos, the Iobakchoi. Iobakchos was a title of Dionysos, a title probably derived from a cry uttered in his worship, and, we remember (p. 85) with sudden delight, the *Gerarae*, the attendants of the Queen, promised in their oath to celebrate, in accordance with ancestral usage, the Iobakcheia.

But the building, and even the traces of an earlier structure that preceded it[3], are of late date; we are on the spot, and yet so far the sanctuary in the Marshes eludes us. But not for long. Digging deeper down, to the level of the ancient road, the excavators came on another and an earlier structure, the triangular precinct marked on the plan, and here at last evidence was found that settled for ever the site of the sanctuary of Dionysos-in-the-Marshes.

The sanctuary, for such we shall immediately see it was, is of triangular shape, and lies substantially lower than the roads by which it is bounded. The sides of the triangle face approximately, North, East and South-West. The precinct is surrounded by an ancient polygonal wall, a portion of which from the South

---

[1] Published and fully discussed by Dr S. Wide, 'Inschrift der Iobakchen,' *A. Mitt.* 1894, p. 248, and see E. Maass, *Orpheus*, p. 16 ff.
[2] *C.I.A.* III. 1159, 1186, 1193, 1197, 1202. See Dr Wide, *op. cit.* p. 1.
[3] See Dr Dörpfeld, *A. Mitt.* xx. 1895, p. 34. The intricacies of this earlier *Bakcheion* do not concern the present argument.

end of the South-West side is shown in Fig. 26.   The material is throughout blue calcareous stone, but the masonry is by no means of uniform excellence or of the same date.   At various periods the

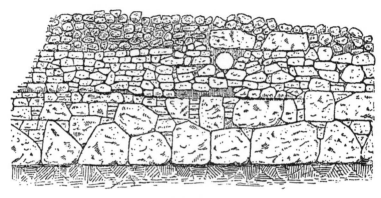

FIG. 26.

wall must have undergone repairs.   The space enclosed is about 560 square metres.   Owing to the fact that the precinct lay deeper than the surrounding roads, sometimes to the extent of two metres, the wall is supported in places by buttresses, only one of which is of good Greek masonry; the rest seem to have been added shortly before the ancient precinct fell into disuse.

A notable point about this precinct wall is that there is no trace of any large entrance-gate.   We expect a gate at the South-West side, where the precinct is skirted by the main road.   Here the wall is well preserved, but there is no trace of any possible gate.   The only feasible place is at the South end of the East wall, where there seems to have been a break, and towards this point, as we shall see, the small temple is orientated.   Here, then, and in all probability here only, was there access to the precinct.

At the North-West corner the excavators came on a structure so far unique in the history of discoveries.   They found a walled-in floor 4·70 m. by 2·80.   This floor is carefully paved with a mixture of pebbles, stone, and cement, and *is inclined to one corner* at an angle of 0·25 m.   At this lowest point there is a hole through the wall enclosing the floor, and outside, let into the pavement, is a large vessel, 0·50 m. in diameter, quadrangular above, round below.   They had found, beyond all possible doubt, what they had never dared to hope they might find, an ancient Greek *wine-press* or *lenos*, and at the finding of that wine-press fled the last lingering misgiving. In Fig. 27 is a view[1] of the

FIG. 27.

wine-press, which shows clearly how it lies just in the corner of the triangular precinct, with its South-West wall (in the front of the picture) abutting on the Panathenaic way. The stucco floor of the wine-press comes out in dead white. In the background can be seen, to the right, the North aisle of the rectangular Bakcheion, and, to the left, the foot of the Areopagus rock.

The wine-press, which is shown in section in Fig. 28, had, like the precinct, had a long history. It had been rebuilt more than once. The paved floors of two successive structures are clearly visible. The upper one is smaller than the lower, and, of course, of later date. It is, however, below the level of the Bakcheion, and must have been underground when the Bakcheion was built. The lower wine-press is at the same level as the *Lesche*, on the opposite side of the road, which is known to be of the 4th century B.C. Under this 4th century wine-press is a pavement

---

[1] I owe this view to the kindness of Mr Percy Droop of Trinity College. It is taken from a point close to the N.W. end of the *Lesche* (Fig. 24).

which must have belonged to a third, yet earlier structure.   It
may be noted that these wine-presses are in every respect exactly
similar to those in use among the Greeks to-day.   The wine-press
within the precinct is not the only one that came to light;
scattered about near at hand were several others.   Two can be

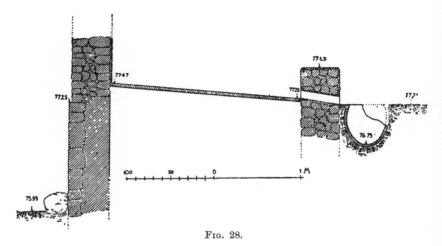

Fig. 28.

seen on the plan in Fig. 35.   It was indeed a place of wine-
presses, a *Lenaion*.

The wine-press in itself would mark the precinct as belonging
to Dionysos, but there was more evidence forthcoming.   In the

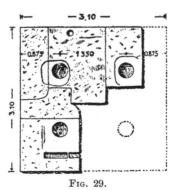

Fig. 29.

centre of the precinct is the foundation in poros stone of a large
altar, 3·10 metres square (Fig. 29).   In this foundation there once

were four holes; three of them remain, and the fourth may be safely supplied. These holes are evidently intended for the supports on which the actual altar-table rested. Such altar-tables are familiar in vase-paintings, and seem to have been in use specially in the cult of Dionysos; they held the wine-jars offered to the god, and baskets of fruit such as those on which the attendants of the Queen took their oath (p. 85). Moreover, the actual altar-slab of just such a table has been found in Attica, and it bears an inscription to Dionysos Auloneus[1]. Yet another important point remains. On the West step of the altar foundation a long groove is sunk in the stone. Its purpose is obvious. Both on the Acropolis and elsewhere in sacred precincts such grooves are found, and they served to contain the bases of *stelae*, on which decrees, dedications, and the like were inscribed. Is it not at least possible that we have here not only the altar on which the Queen took her oath, but the groove in which was set up the very stele on which it was inscribed, the stele which stood 'alongside of the altar' (παρὰ τὸν βωμόν)?

We have, then, a precinct secluded from the main road; within it, open to the air, a great altar. But inside this precinct not a single inscription nor any sort of votive offering has come to light. In a precinct so important this at first sight seems strange. The explanation lies to hand. Votive offerings are meant to be seen, meant to show forth the piety of the worshipper as well as the glory of the god. Was it worth while to dedicate an offering in a precinct that was open but for one day in the whole year? Apparently not. This was essentially a 'mystery' sanctuary, with no touch of the museum.

In the sanctuary of Dionysos-in-the-Marshes we expect not only precinct and altar but an actual temple, the existence of which we know, not from Thucydides, but from the scholiast[2] on the *Frogs* of Aristophanes. Commenting on the word 'marsh' he says, 'a sacred place of Dionysos, in which there is a dwelling and a temple of the god. Callimachus in the *Hekale* says,

> 'To him, Limnaios, do they keep the feast
> With choral dances.'

[1] *A. Mitt.* v. 116.
[2] Schol. ad Ar. *Ran.* 216 Λίμνη τόπος ἱερὸς Διονύσου ἐν ᾧ καὶ οἶκος καὶ νεὼς τοῦ θεοῦ Καλλίμαχος ἐν Ἑκάλῃ
Λιμναίῳ δὲ χοροστάδας ἦγον ἑορτάς.

The 'dwelling' may be some building that contained the wine-press; the temple happily has been found, and its position in relation to the precinct is strange and significant.

The foundations of the temple came to light in the South corner of the precinct. It is of small size (3·96 by 3·40 m.), and consists of a quadrangular cella and a narrow pronaos. From its small size it seems unlikely that the pronaos had any columns. The masonry is very ancient. The walls are polygonal, and the blocks of calcareous stone of which they are made are on the South-West side unusually large. In the foundations of the side-walls a few *poros* blocks occur. There are no steps serving as foundation to either cella or pronaos. From this Professor Dörpfeld concludes that in all probability this temple is earlier than the temple of Dionysos Eleuthereus, close to the *skenè* of the theatre. The temple of Eleuthereus belonged to the time of Peisistratos; it is more carefully built than the one newly discovered, and it has one step. Early though the newly discovered building undoubtedly is, it was preceded by a yet earlier structure, the walls of which, marked on the plan, lie beneath its foundations.

Quite exceptional is the relation of the temple to the precinct. It does not lie in the middle, and is, moreover, separated from the inner part of the precinct by a wall and a door that could be closed. This separating wall is however apparently later than the temple, which possibly at one time stood free within the precinct. The separating wall is only explicable on ritual grounds. It made it possible for the temple to be accessible all the year round, whereas the precinct, save for one day in the year, was closed.

Are we to give to the ancient sanctuary the name *Lenaion*? To the sanctuary itself probably not. The meaning of *Lenaion*, it would seem, is not 'sanctuary of the god Lenaios,' but rather 'place of the wine-press.' It is noticeable that writers who could themselves have seen the sanctuary never call it *Lenaion*. Thucydides[1], the writer of the oration *against Neaera*[2], be he Demosthenes or Apollodorus, and again Phanodemus[3], as quoted by Athenaeus, all speak of it as the sanctuary of *Dionysos-in-the-*

---

[1] Thucyd. II. 15 τὸ ἐν Λίμναις Διονύσου.
[2] c. *Neaer.* 76 τὸ ἱερὸν τοῦ Διονύσου ἐν Λίμναις.
[3] Phanodemus ap. Athen. XI. 465 A τὸ ἱερὸν τοῦ ἐν Λίμναις Διονύσου.

Marshes. Isaeus[1] calls it the Dionysion-in-the-Marshes. On the
other hand, when contemporary authors speak of the dramatic
contest which was held not in honour of Dionysos Eleuthereus
but at the older Dionysia, they speak of the contest as *at* or *on*
the Lenaion, never as *in-the-Marshes.* The natural conclusion is
that the name *Lenaion* is applicable to the place where the
contests actually took place, namely to the ancient Orchestra
and perhaps its immediate neighbourhood. The district of the
wine-presses naturally had its dancing place, and that dancing
place was called the Lenaion. To this day the peasants of Greece
use for their festival-dances the village threshing-floor.

In the theatre of Eleuthereus Dr Dörpfeld[2] has given back to
us the old orchestra. He has shown us deep down below the successive Graeco-Roman and Roman stages the old circular orchestra
built of polygonal masonry (Fig. 16). On this old orchestra, with
only wooden seats for the spectators, were acted, we now know,
the dramas of Aeschylus, Sophocles, Euripides, nay tradition[3] even
says, and we have no cause to doubt its veracity, that Thespis
was the first (in 586 B.C.) to exhibit a play in the 'city' contest
(ἐν ἄστει).

But ancient though it was, before it, as we have seen, came
the orchestra in the Limnae. Dr Dörpfeld had hoped that his
excavations would give back this orchestra too; this hope has not
been fulfilled. Traces have been found of a circular structure on
the South slope of the Areopagus and are marked on the plan
(Fig. 46), but they are of uncertain date, and, if they mark the
site of any ancient building, it is probably that of the Odeion of
Agrippa. The old orchestra lay at the North-West corner of the
Areopagos.

Tradition records the beginning of the contests 'in the city,'
i.e. in the theatre of Eleuthereus, but the beginnings of the other
festivals, the Lenaia and the Chytroi, held in the Limnae, are
lost in the mists before. The two are in all probability but

---

[1] Is. *Or.* VIII. 35 τὸ ἐν Λίμναις Διονύσιον. For these references see Dr Dörpfeld,
'Lenaion,' *A. Mitt.* 1895, xx. p. 368.
[2] For the fullest account of this orchestra see Prof. Dörpfeld, *Das Griechische
Theater,* p. 27.
[3] In the *Parian Chronicle,* ἀφ' οὗ Θέσπις ὁ ποιητὴς [ὑπεκρίνα]το πρῶτος, ὃς ἐδίδαξε
[δρ]ᾶ[μα ἐν ἄ]στ[ει. The restoration ἐν ἄστει seems certain.

different names for the same festival, or rather the Chytroi is
the whole ceremony of the third day of the Anthesteria and
Lenaia the name given to the dramatic part of the ceremonies.
But though we do not know the beginning, and though, as will
presently be seen, the 'Pot-Contests' went back in all probability
to a time before the coming of Dionysos, we have hints as to
how the end came, how the splendour and convenience of the
great theatre of Eleuthereus gradually obscured and absorbed the
primitive contests of the orchestra in the Limnae.

It was, we know, the great statesman Lycurgus who, in the
4th century B.C., built the first permanent stone stage in the
theatre and made the seats for the spectators as we see them now.
So pleased was he, it would seem, with his theatre that he thought
it useless and senseless to have plays acted elsewhere. Accordingly
in the *Lives of the Ten Orators*[1] we learn that Lycurgus introduced
laws, and among them one about comic writers 'to hold a performance at the Chytroi, a competitive one, in the theatre,' and 'to record
the victor as a victor in the city,' which had formerly not been
allowed. He thus revived the performance which had fallen into
disuse.

Lycurgus meant well we may be sure, but he was a Butad[2], he
ought to have known better than to pluck up an old festival
by the roots like that and think to foster it by transplantation.
The end was certain; the old precinct, deserted by its festivals, was
bit by bit forgotten, overgrown, and at last in part built over by
the new Iobakchoi.

The precinct had lost prestige by the time of Pausanias[3].
Had the temple of Dionysos-in-the-Marshes been above ground
he would assuredly not have passed it by. Near to where the
precinct once was he saw a building, a circular or semi-circular
one, which may have been a last Roman reminiscence of the
orchestra, and still of note though it did not occupy the same site;
he notes 'a theatre which they call the Odeion.' It is probable
that this was the theatre built by Agrippa and mentioned by

---

[1] Ps. Plut. *Vit. X. Orat.* 6 εἰσήνεγκε δὲ καὶ νόμους τὸν περὶ τῶν κωμῳδῶν ἀγῶνα
τοῖς Χύτροις ἐπιτελεῖν ἐφάμιλλον ἐν τῷ θεάτρῳ, καὶ τὸν νικήσαντα εἰς ἄστυ καταλέγεσθαι,
πρότερον οὐκ ἐξὸν, ἀναλαμβάνων τὸν ἀγῶνα ἐκλελοιπότα.

[2] Ps. Plut. *Vit. X. Orat.*

[3] Paus. I. 8. 6 τὸ θέατρον ὃ καλοῦσιν ᾠδεῖον.

Philostratos[1] as 'the theatre in the Kerameikos, which goes by the name of the Agrippeion.'

Before leaving the sanctuary in-the-Marshes, a word must be said as to the Anthesteria or, as Thucydides calls it, 'the more ancient Dionysiac Festival.' I have tried elsewhere[2] to show in detail that the Dionysiac element in the Anthesteria was only a thin upper layer beneath which lay a ritual of immemorial antiquity, which had for its object the promotion of fertility by means of the placation of ghosts or heroes. On the first day, if I am right, the *Pithoigia* was an Opening not only of wine-jars but of grave-jars; the second, the *Choes*, was a feast not only of Cups but of Libations (χοαί); the third, the *Chytroi*, not only a Pot-feast, but a feast of Holes in the ground and of the solemn dismissal of Keres back to the lower world. That the collective name of the whole feast *Anthesteria* did not primarily mean the festival of those who 'did the flowers,' but rather of those who 'revoked the ghosts[3].'

But in trying to distinguish the two strata, the under stratum of ghosts, the upper of Dionysos, I never doubted that the Pot Contest on the day of the *Chytroi* belonged to Dionysos. Dionysos and the 'origin of the drama' are canonically connected. It has remained, therefore, something of a mystery how Dionysos, late comer as he was, contrived to possess himself of the ancient ghost-festival and impose his dramatic contests on a ritual sub-stratum apparently so uncongenial. Religions are accommodating enough, but some sort of analogy or possible bridge from one to the other is necessary for affiliation.

The difficulty disappears at once if we accept Professor Ridgeway's[4] recent theory as to the origin of tragedy. The drama according to him is not 'Dorian,' and, save for the one element of the Satyric play, not Dionysiac. It took its rise in mimetic dances at the tombs of local heroes. When Dionysos came to Athens with his Satyr attendants he would find the Pot-Contests as part

---

[1] Philostr. *Vit. Soph.* II. 5. 4 τὸ ἐν τῷ Κεραμεικῷ θέατρον ὃ δὴ ἐπωνόμασται Ἀγριππεῖον. For the whole question of the Odeion which, save for its possible identity in site with the old orchestra, does not concern us, see Dr Dörpfeld, 'Die verschiedenen Odeien in Athen,' *A. Mitt.* XVII. 1892, p. 352.

[2] *Prolegomena to the Study of Greek Religion*, Chapter II., The Anthesteria.

[3] Dr Verrall, *J. H. S.* XX. 115.

[4] *Journal of Hellenic Studies* XXIV. p. xxxix. 1904.

of the funeral ritual of the Anthesteria.   He added to the festival wine and the Satyrs.   Small wonder that comedy, as in the *Frogs*, was at home in the Underworld, and could in all piety parody a funeral[1] on the stage.

Thucydides has given us four examples of sanctuaries outside the *polis* which are 'towards that part' of it, but again, as in the first clause, he seems to feel that if he has spoken the truth it is not the whole truth, so he saves himself from misunderstanding by an additional clause, '*and other ancient sanctuaries are placed here.*'

It would be idle to try and give a complete list of all the sanctuaries that were situated in this particular region, still more idle to decide of what particular sanctuaries Thucydides was thinking.   The precinct of Aglauros and the Anakeion on the North side, the sanctuary of the Semnae and the Amyneion on the West, the sanctuary of Aphrodite Pandemos and that of Themis on the West and South-West are all 'towards' the approach.   Three out of these, the Amyneion, the sanctuary of the Semnae, and the sanctuary of Aphrodite Pandemos, are of such interest in themselves and so essential to the forming of a picture of the sanctities of ancient Athens that a word must be said of each.

The Amyneion.   The Amyneion, or sanctuary of Amynos[2], is known to us only through monumental evidence, brought to light in the recent excavations.   Its discovery is one of the things that make us feel suddenly how much of popular faith we, relying as we must almost wholly on literature, may have utterly lost.

If after leaving the precinct of Dionysos in-the-Marshes we follow the main road for about 35 metres, we come on a precinct (Fig. 30) of much smaller size and of quadrangular shape, which abuts on the road and along the North side of which a narrow foot-path leads up to the Acropolis.   The precinct-walls are of hard blue calcareous stone from the Acropolis and neighbouring hills, and the masonry is good polygonal.   The entrance-gate (A),

---

[1] It seems to me possible that the transition may have been helped as regards the word Lenaion by the fact that the Greek λην∘́ς means *coffin* as well as *wine-press*. The λην∘́ς like the πίθος could be used for purposes widely diverse.

[2] A. Koerte, 'Bezirk eines Heilgottes,' *A. Mitt.* 1893, XVIII. pl. xi.; A. Koerte, 'Ausgrabungen am Westabhange IV. Das Heiligtum des Amynos,' *A. Mitt.* 1896, XXI. p. 286, pl. xi.

which has been rebuilt in Roman times, is at the North-West corner. A little to the East of the middle of the precinct, and

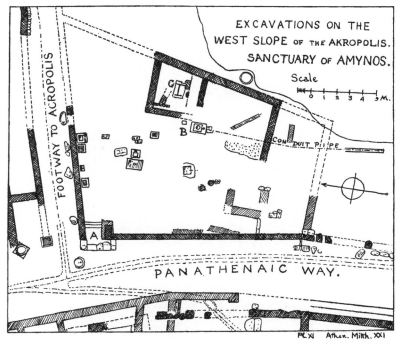

FIG. 30.

manifestly of great importance, is a well (B). The natural supply of this well was reinforced by a conduit-pipe, which leads direct into it from the great water-course of Peisistratos, which will later (p. 119) be described. Near the well are remains of a small hero-chapel, and within this was found the lower part of a marble sacrificial table (C), decorated with two snakes. The masonry of the precinct wall, the well, and the shrine all point to a date at the time of Peisistratos. Even before the limits of this precinct were fairly made out the excavators came upon a number of frag-ments of votive offerings of a familiar type. Such are reliefs representing parts of the human body, breasts and the like, votive snakes, and reliefs representing worshippers approaching a god of the usual Asklepios type. Conspicuous among these was a fine well-preserved relief (Fig. 31), depicting a man holding a huge leg, very clearly marked with a varicose vein, exactly where, doctors say, a varicose vein should be.   The inscription[1] above the figure

Fɪɢ. 31.

is unfortunately so effaced that no facts emerge save that the dedicator, the man who holds the leg, was the son of a certain

[1]
ων τευξα-
—ων σεμνοτάτην.
Λυσιμαχι]δῆς Λυσιμάχου ᾿Αχαρνε[ύς.
See Dr Koerte's discussion of the relief, *A. Mitt.* 1893, p. 235.

Lysimachos, and was of the deme Acharnae. The style of the letters and of the sculpture dates the monument as of about the first half of the 4th century B.C. It was clear enough that the excavators had come on the precinct of a god of healing, and a few decades ago the precinct would have been labelled without more ado as 'sacred to As-klepios.' We should then have been left with the curious pro-blem, Why had Asklepios two precincts, one on the South, one on the West ? We know that Asklepios made his tri-umphant entry into the great precinct on the South slope in 421 B.C.; if he had had a pre-cinct on the West slope since the days of Peisistratos, why did he leave it ?

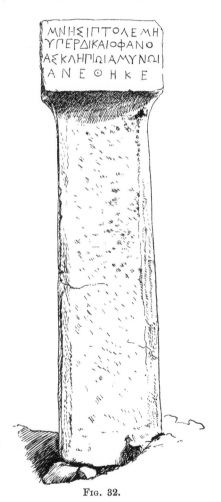

FIG. 32.

But now-a-days in the matter of ascription we pro-ceed more cautiously. We know that votive-reliefs of the 'Asklepios' type are offered to almost any local hero, that local heroes anywhere and every-where are hero-healers[1]. Hence local hero-healers were gradual-ly absorbed and effaced by the most successful of their number, Asklepios. In literature we hear little of the hero-cult of an Amphiaraos, but his local shrine went on down to late days at Oropus. Fortunately in our precinct we have inscriptions that leave us no doubt. On a stele[2] (Fig. 32) found there we have an inscription as follows:

[1] See my *Prolegomena*, p. 349.
[2] Koerte, *A. Mitt.* 1896, xxi. p. 295 Μνησιπτολέμη ὑπὲρ Δικαιοφάνου[ς] Ἀσκληπιῷ Ἀμύνῳ ἀνέθηκε.

'Mnesiptolemè on behalf of Dikaiophanes dedicated (this) to Asklepios Amynos.'

At first we seem no further; we have the familiar Asklepios worshipped under the title of Amynos, Protector, Defender. A second inscription[1], however, makes it certain that *Amynos* is not merely an adjective attached to Asklepios, but the cultus title of a person separate from Asklepios. This inscription, of the latter half of the 4th century B.C., is in honour of certain persons who had been benefactors of the *thiasos* (ὀργεῶνες) of *Amynos and of Asklepios and of Dexion*. We know who Dexion was; he was Sophocles, heroized, and he, the mortal, came last on the list. Sophocles had a shrine apart, or it may be a separate shrine within the larger one. The same inscription[2] goes on to order that the honorary decree was to be 'engraved on two stone stelae, and these to be set up, the one in the sanctuary of Dexion, the other in that of Amynos and Asklepios.'

Sophocles[3] though, to us, he is first in remembrance, comes last in ritual precedence; Amynos is first. The history of the little shrine is instructive. Not later than Peisistratos, and how much earlier we do not know, the worship was set up of a local hero with the title Protector, *Amynos*. At some time or other, perhaps shortly after the pestilence at Athens, which the local Protector had been powerless to avert, it was thought well to call in a greater Healer-Hero, Asklepios, who meanwhile had attained in the Peloponnesos to enormous prestige. The experiment was tried carefully and quietly in the little precinct. Amynos kept his own precedence. No one's feelings are hurt; the snake of the Peloponnesos is merely affiliated to the local Athenian hero-snake, the same offerings are due to both, the *pelanoi*, the votive limbs. But the new-comer is too strong; Asklepios waxes, Amynos wanes—into an adjective. Asklepios outgrows the little precinct and betakes himself to a new and grander sanctuary on the South slope.

The precinct and worship of Amynos, though it has no mention in literature, is preserved to us perhaps through its association

[1] Koerte, *op. cit.* p. 299...δεδόχθαι τοῖς ὀργεῶσι ἐπειδή εἰσιν ἄνδρες ἀγαθοὶ περὶ τὰ κοινὰ τῶν ὀργεώνων τοῦ Ἀμύνου καὶ τοῦ Ἀσκληπιοῦ καὶ τοῦ Δεξίονος... .
[2] line 15 ἀναγράψαι δὲ τόδε τὸ ψήφισμα ἐν στήλαις λιθίναις δυοῖν καὶ στῆσαι τὴν μὲν ἐν τῷ το[ῦ] Δεξίονος ἱερῷ τὴν δὲ [ἐ]ν τῷ το(ῦ) Ἀμύνου καὶ Ἀσκληπιοῦ.
[3] For the worship of Sophocles, see my *Prolegomena*, p. 346.

with the dominant worship of Asklepios; but Amynos was probably only one among many heroes who had their chapels and their family worships scattered along the main road of the city where countless little buildings remain unidentified (Fig. 35). If the supposition suggested above (p. 99) be correct these local heroes must have had choral dances about their tombs, those choral dances affiliated by the late-comer Dionysos, and ultimately leading to the development of the drama. At the festival of the Anthesteria these local ghosts would be summoned from their tombs on the day of the Pithoigia; on the day of the Chytroi they would be fed and their descendants would hold a wake with revels and dancings.

The Sanctuary of the Semnae Theai or Venerable Goddesses. The site of this sanctuary is practically certain. Euripides[1] in the *Electra* makes the Erinyes, when they are about to become Semnae, descend into a chasm of the earth near to the Areopagos. Near to the Areopagos there is one chasm and one only, that is the deep fissure on the North-East side, the spot where tradition has long placed the cave of the Semnae[2]. A cave they needed, for they were under-world goddesses. Their ritual I have discussed in detail elsewhere[3]; here it need only be noted that it was of great antiquity and had all the characteristic marks of a chthonic cult. As under-world goddesses the Venerable Ones bore the title also of *Arai*, Imprecations; they were for cursing as well as blessing; the hill it is now generally acknowledged took its name from them rather than from the war-god Ares. Orestes it will be remembered[4] came to the Areopagos to be purified from his mother's blood, and he found the people celebrating the Choes; he found them, if our topography be correct, close by, in the precinct of Dionysos-in-the-Marshes.

The Sanctuary of Aphrodite Pandemos. Harpocration[5] in explaining the title *Pandemos* tells us that Apollodorus in the sixth book of his treatise *About the Gods* said that this was 'the name given at Athens to the goddess whose worship had been established

---

[1] Eur. *El.* 1271. [2] *Myth. and Mon. Anc. Athens*, II. p. 554.
[3] *Prolegomena*, pp. 239—253. [4] Athen. x. 437.
[5] Harp. *s.v.* Πάνδημος 'Αφροδίτη...'Απολλόδωρος ἐν τῷ περὶ Θεῶν πάνδημόν φησιν 'Αθήνῃσι κληθῆναι τὴν ἀφιδρυθεῖσαν περὶ τὴν ἀρχαίαν ἀγοράν....

somewhere near the ancient agora.' His conjecture that the goddess was called Pandemos because all the people collected in the agora need not detain us, but the topographical statement coming from an author who knew his subject like Apollodorus, is important. We have to seek the sanctuary of Pandemos somewhere on or close to the West slope of the Acropolis, somewhere near the great square which as we shall see (p. 131) stood in front of the ancient well-house and formed the ancient agora.

Pausanias[1] mentions the worship of Aphrodite Pandemos in a sentence of the most tantalizing vagueness. After leaving the Asklepieion he notes a temple of Themis and in front of it a monument to Hippolytus. He then tells at length the story of Phaedra and next goes on 'When Theseus united the various Athenian demes into one people he introduced the worship of Aphrodite Pandemos and Peitho. The old images were not there in my time, but those I saw were the work of no obscure artists.' Immediately after he passes to the sanctuary of Ge Kourotrophos and Demeter Chloe and then straight to the citadel.

Of the actual sanctuary of Aphrodite Pandemos not a trace has been found. From the account of Pausanias coupled with that of Harpocration we should expect it to be somewhere below the sanctuary of Ge and above the fountain Enneakrounos, near which was the ancient agora, and of course outside the Pelargikon. When the West slope of the Acropolis was excavated[2] in the upper layers of earth about 40 statuettes of Aphrodite were found, and these must have belonged to the sanctuary. Inscriptions[3] relating to her worship were found built into a mediaeval fortification wall near Beule's Gate. These, as not being *in situ*, cannot be used as topographical evidence, but they give us important information as to the character of the worship of Pandemos.

The first[4] of these inscriptions (Fig. 33) dates about the beginning of the fifth century B.C. '[...]dorus dedicated me

---

[1] Paus. I. 22. 3. [2] Dörpfeld, *A. Mitt.* 1896, p. 511.
[3] Foucart, *Bull. de Corr. Hell.* 1889, p. 157.
[4] The facsimile is from Δελτίον 1889, p. 127. The inscription reads as follows:
...]δωρος μ' ἀνέθηκ' 'Αφροδίτην δῶρον ἀπαρχήν.
Πότνια τῶν ἀγαθῶν τῶ[ι] σὺ δὸς ἀφθον[ί]αν.
οἵ τε λέγ[ου]σι λόγους ἀδίκως ψευδᾶς κ...εκ...
It is discussed with the two that follow by Mr Foucart, *Bull. de Corr. Hell.* 1889, p. 157.

to Aphrodite a gift of first fruits, Lady do thou grant him abundance of good things. But they who unrighteously say false things and....' Unfortunately here the inscription breaks off so the scandal will remain for ever a secret. Aphrodite, it is to be noted, is prayed to as a giver of increase. She does not seem yet to have got her title of Pandemos, but as this occurs in the two other inscriptions found with this one, and they probably all three came from the same sanctuary, this Aphrodite is almost certainly she who became Pandemos.

ΔΕΛΤ.ΑΡΧ. V 1889 p 127

FIG. 33.

The second inscription (Fig. 34), dating about the middle of the 4th century B.C., is carved on an architrave adorned with

Δελτ. Ἀρχ. V 1889 p 128

FIG. 34.

a frieze of doves carrying a fillet. The architrave is broken midway. Only the left-hand half is represented in the figure. This inscription[1] again is partly metrical, forming an elegiac couplet.

> 'This for thee, O great and holy Pandemos Aphr[odite,
> We adorn with gifts, our statues.'

Beneath in prose and in smaller letters come the names of the dedicators. Pandemos is here quite plainly the official title of the goddess.

[1]   Τόνδε σοί, ὦ μεγάλη σεμνὴ Πάνδημε Ἀφρ[οδίτη]
       [κοσ]μοῦμεν δώροις εἰκόσιν ἡμετέραις

    Ἀρχῖνος Ἀλυπήτου Σκαμβωνίδης, Μενεκράτεια Δεξικράτους
    Ἰκαριέως θυγάτηρ, ἱέρεια τῆς [Ἀφροδίτης],...
    ...Δ]εξικράτους Ἰκαριέως θυγάτηρ, Ἀρχίνου δὲ μήτηρ.

For discussion of this inscription and the nature of the building dedicated, see Dr Kawerau, 'Die Pandemos-Weihung auf der Akropolis' (*A. Mitt.* 1905), which through his kindness reached me after the above was written.

The third and latest inscription[1] is carved on a stele of Hymettus marble. It is exactly dated (283 B.C.) by the archon's name, the elder Euthios. It records a decree made while a woman called Hegesipyle was priestess. The decree, which is too long to be here quoted in full, ordains that the *astynomoi* should at the time of the procession in honour of Aphrodite Pandemos 'provide a dove for the purification of the temple, should have the altars anointed, should give a coat of pitch to the roof and wash the statues and prepare a purple robe.'

Aphrodite Pandemos was a 'great and holy goddess,' giver of increase. She was no private divinity of the courtesan; the second inscription tells us that she was worshipped by a married woman, who is her priestess. It is literature and not ritual that has cast a slur on the title Pandemos; the state honoured both her and Ourania alike 'according to ancestral custom.' Plato[2] in his beautiful reckless way will have it that because there are two Loves there are two Goddesses, 'the elder one having no mother, who is the Heavenly Aphrodite, the daughter of Ouranos; to her we give the title Ourania, the younger, who is the daughter of Zeus and Dione, and her we call "Of-all-the-People," Pandemos.'

The real truth was that Aphrodite came to the Greeks from the East and like most Semitic divinities she was not only a duality but a trinity.

When Pausanias[3] was at Thebes he saw the images of this ancient Oriental trinity and he knew whence they had come. 'There are wooden images of Aphrodite at Thebes so ancient that it is said they were dedicated by Harmonia and that they were made out of the wooden figure-heads of the ships of Cadmus. One of them is called Heavenly, another Of-all-the-People, and the third the Turner-Away.' The threefold Aphrodite came from the Semitic East bearing three Semitic titles: she was the Queen of Heaven[4], she was the Lady of all the People, Ourania and

<hr>

[1]

ἡ πομπὴ τῆι ᾿Αφροδίτηι τῆι Πανδή-
μωι παρασκευάζειν εἰς κάθαρσι[ν
τ]οῦ ἱεροῦ περιστέραν καὶ περιαλε[ῖ-
ψαι] τοὺς βωμοὺς καὶ πιττῶσαι τὰ[ς
ὀροφὰς] καὶ λοῦσαι τὰ ἕδη παρασκευ-
άσαι δὲ κα]ὶ πορφύραν ὀλκὴν ⊢ ⊦ [⊢.

See *B.C.H.* 1889, p. 157, and *Myth. and Mon. Anc. Athens*, p. 331.
[2] Plat. *Symp.* 180 D. For Aphrodite Ourania, see *Myth. and Mon. Anc. Athens*, p. 211.   [3] Paus. IX. 16. 3.
[4] I follow M. Victor Bérard, *Origine des cultes Arcadiens*, p. 142. Ourania is

Pandemos, what the third title was which the Greeks translated into Apostrophia we do not know; as already noted it took slight hold. At Megalopolis[1] we see how the third title of the trinity faded. There close to the house where was an image of Ammon made like a Herm and with the horns of a ram, there—significant conjunction—was a sanctuary of Aphrodite in ruins, with the front part only left and it had three images, 'one named Ourania the other Pandemos, *the third had no particular name.*' So it was that the Greeks lost the trinity and kept, all they needed, the duality.

The Greeks themselves always knew quite well whence came their Heavenly Aphrodite, she of Paphos, and she of Kythera. Herodotus[2] is explicit. He is telling how some of the Scythians in their passage through Palestine from Egypt pillaged the sanctuary of Aphrodite Ourania at Ascalon. 'This sanctuary,' he says, 'I found on enquiry is the most ancient of all those that are dedicated to this goddess, for the sanctuary in Cyprus had its origin from thence, as the Cyprians themselves say, and that in Kythera was founded by Phenicians who came from this part of Syria.' Pausanias[3] says 'the first to worship Ourania were the Assyrians, next to them were the dwellers in Paphos of Cyprus, and the Phenicians of Ascalon in Palestine. And the inhabitants of Kythera learnt the worship from the Phenicians.'

The Oriental origin[4] of Ourania, Queen of Heaven, the armed goddess, the *Virgo Caelestis*, was patent to all; but Aphrodite in her more human earthly aspect, as Pandemos, goddess of the

---

'Queen of Heaven,' מלכת־הֹשמים, as in the Hebrew scriptures, Jerem. vii. 18, xliv. 18—20. Pandemos is רבת הארץ, lady of the land. I have ventured above, p. 54, to suggest that to the armed Ourania, the *Virgo Caelestis*, we owe at least some elements in the armed Athena.

[1] Paus. VIII. 32. 2.
[2] Herod. I. 105. The name Kythera is Semitic (כתרת); see M. Victor Bérard, *Les Phéniciens et l'Odyssée*, p. 427. *Kythera* means a headdress, a tiara, and its Greek 'doublette' is Skandeia.
[3] Paus. I. 14. 7.
[4] We have incidentally curious evidence of the association of Kourotrophos with the Oriental Aphrodite. An inscription (*C.I.A.* III. 411) found on a Turkish wall near the temple of Nike mentions the entrance to a chapel of Blaute and Kourotrophos (εἴσοδος πρὸς σηκὸν Βλαύτης καὶ Κουροτρόφου). Lydus (*de Mens.* I. 21), on the authority of Phlegon, tells us that Blatta was 'a title of Aphrodite among the Phenicians' (καὶ βλάττα δέ, ἐξ ἧς τὰ βλάττια λέγομεν, ὄνομα Ἀφροδίτης, ἐστι κατὰ τοὺς Φοίνικας ὡς ὁ Φλέγων ἐν τῷ περὶ ἑορτῶν φησί). He does not tell us,—what is obvious enough,—that Blaute and Blatta are Greek attempts to reproduce Baalat (בַּעֲלָת). Blaute is but Aphrodite-Pandemos, Lady, Baalat of the People.

people and of all increase, was so like Kourotrophos, like Demeter, that she might easily be thought of as indigenous. Yet her ritual betrays her. For the purification of her sanctuary we have seen there was ordered a dove. Instinctively we remember that when Mary Virgin[1] went up to the temple of Jerusalem for her purification she must take with her 'a pair of turtle-doves or two young pigeons.' In the statuettes of Paphos, Aphrodite holds a dove in her hand; the coins of Salamis in Cyprus are stamped with the dove[2]. At the Phenician Eryx when the festival of the Anagogia[3] came round, and Aphrodite Astarte went back to her home in Libya, the doves went with her, and when they came back at the *Katagogia*, a white multitude, among them was one with feathers of red gold, and she was Aphrodite.

---

[1] Luke ii. 24.
[2] Mr E. Babelon, *Monnaies des Phéniciens*, cxxv.
[3] Æl. *Nat. Anim.* iv. 2; see M. Victor Bérard, *Cultes Arcadiens*, p. 106.

CHAPTER IV.

THE SPRING KALLIRRHOË-ENNEAKROUNOS 'NEAR' THE CITADEL.

καὶ τῇ κρήνῃ τῇ νῦν μὲν τῶν τυράννων οὕτω σκευασάντων Ἐννεακρούνῳ καλουμένῃ, τὸ δὲ πάλαι φανερῶν τῶν πηγῶν οὐσῶν Καλλιρρόῃ ὠνομασμένῃ—ἐκείνῃ τε ἐγγὺς οὔσῃ τὰ πλείστου ἄξια ἐχρῶντο, καὶ νῦν ἔτι ἀπὸ τοῦ ἀρχαίου πρό τε γαμικῶν καὶ ἐς ἄλλα τῶν ἱερῶν νομίζεται τῷ ὕδατι χρῆσθαι.

THE argument now stands as follows. As evidence that the old city was *the present citadel with the addition of what is below it towards about South* Thucydides has adduced two facts: 1st, that *the sanctuaries are in the citadel, those of other deities as well (as the Goddess)*; 2nd, that *those that are outside are placed towards this part of the city more (than elsewhere)*. Instances of such outside shrines are *the sanctuary of Zeus Olympios and the Pythion, and the sanctuary of Ge, and that of Dionysos-in-the-Marshes.* This last is defined, to prevent confusion with the later sanctuary of Dionysos Eleuthereus, as the scene of the earlier Dionysia. Finally, *other ancient sanctuaries also* (not named) are placed here.

We next come to the third fact adduced as evidence, namely, a statement as to the position of the ancient city spring, as follows: '*And the spring which is now called "Nine-Spouts," from the form given it by the despots, but which formerly, when the sources were open, was named Fair-Fount—this spring* (I say) *being near, they used for the most important purposes, and even now it is still the custom in consequence of the ancient* (habit) *to use the water before weddings and for other sacred purposes.*' Was ever argument stated in fashion more odd, involved, and utterly Thucydidean?

A spring which was once called Kallirrhoë and now Enneakrounos is 'near,' *i.e.* is near the ancient city as above defined, and is now used for weddings and the like. Why does Thucydides, who is 'least of all mortals a gossip,' tell us about the water and the weddings? Why refer to the history of the fountain at all? Because, as in the case of the Anthesteria, the reference to things ancient is part of his argument. The train of thought is this. The water of Nine-Spouts is now used for weddings. Why? On the face of it there seems no particular reason. The fountain 'Nine-Spouts' has water enough and to spare. But the fountain 'Nine-Spouts' was not always there, it replaced 'Fair-Fount,' and this spring the ancient Athenians used only for 'most important' purposes. Again, why? Well, clearly because there was not enough of it for general use. It was 'near,' and yet they reserved it for special purposes. We may gather, then, from the account of Thucydides, though he does not expressly state it, the despots not only changed the name but increased the 'water supply[1].'

As to where the spring was, save that it is 'near,' Thucydides says absolutely nothing. It might be North, East, South, or West. We who have followed him step by step down the western slope, from the Olympieion and Pythion to the sanctuary of Ge and to the sanctuary of Dionysos-in-the-Marshes, expect to find 'Nine-Spouts' somewhere near these sites, somewhere in the depression enclosed by Acropolis, Pnyx, and Areopagos. But we must bear in mind that this expectation is based on *our* identification of the previous sanctuaries, not on any words of Thucydides about the spring.

But when we ask, as we inevitably must, where did *Pausanias* see the famous fountain, we are in better case. Pausanias[2] saw 'Nine-Spouts' near to the Odeion, and the Odeion he saw immediately after the statues of Harmodios and Aristogeiton, on the slope of the Areopagos. Immediately after the Enneakrounos, 'beyond the fountain,' as he says, Pausanias[3] saw the temples of Demeter and Kore, which can scarcely be separated from the Thesmophorion on the Pnyx. Somewhere adjacent to both Pnyx

---

[1] For what can here be deduced from the text apart from new archeological material, see Dr Verrall, *Class. Rev.* 1900, p. 277.

[2] Paus. I. 14. 1 πλησίον δέ ἐστι κρήνη, καλοῦσι δὲ αὐτὴν 'Εννεάκρουνον, οὕτω κοσμηθεῖσαν ὑπὸ Πεισιστράτου. Between the statues of Harmodios and Aristogeiton (I. 8. 5) and the Odeion (I. 8. 6) there is no connecting particle. This often happens in Pausanias when things in immediate juxtaposition are described. Traces of curved foundations of Roman date which may mark the site of the Odeion are shown in Prof. Dörpfeld's plan (Fig. 46), but as the identification is conjectural I prefer not to use it as an argument.

[3] Paus. I. 14. 1 ναοὶ δὲ ὑπὲρ τὴν κρήνην ὁ μὲν Δήμητρος πεποίηται καὶ Κόρης.

and Areopagos we should, from Pausanias, expect to find 'Nine-Spouts,' and there find it we shall.

It is fortunate for us that Thucydides was so explicit about the fountain. He gives us not merely a fountain called Fair-Fount but a fountain called Fair-Fount that was turned into Nine-Spouts. This is fortunate, because the word translated 'Fair-Fount,' *Kallirrhoë*, is a term so general that it might be applied to almost any spring. If in travelling through Greece to-day you stop to drink from a spring and ask your guide its name, he will, three times out of four, tell you it is *Mavromati*, *Black-Eye*, because that is a term so general as to be safely applicable. So at Athens there was, certainly in later days and possibly even in the time of Thucydides, another Kallirrhoë far away on the Ilissus. As Socrates, in the *Axiochos*[1], was going out towards Kynosarges and had reached the Ilissos he heard some one shouting to him, and turning round he saw Kleinias running towards Kallirrhoë. Clearly this was another Kallirrhoë, not the one near the Pnyx. How this duplication of Kallirrhoës at Athens arose will later (p. 143) be considered. The Kallirrhoë we are in search of is the Fair-Fount *which became the Nine-Spouts*, that and no other.

It is worth noticing how quickly the spring lost its old name. People were, no doubt, very proud of the new *Nine-Spouts*. Herodotus[2] naively assumes that in the days of the Pelasgians *Fair-Fount* was called *Nine-Spouts*. The Athenians said that their expulsion of the Pelasgians from Attica was justified, for 'the Pelasgians who were settled under Hymettus used to make excursions thence and do lawless deeds. Their daughters used constantly to go to the Enneakrounos for water, for at that time the Greeks had no household servants, and whenever they came the Pelasgians used to offer them violence out of insolence and contempt.' There must have been people alive in the days of Thucydides whose fathers remembered the change made by the

---

[1] Plat. *Axioch.* I. § 364 Ἐξιόντι μοι ἐς Κυνόσαργες καὶ γενομένῳ [μοι] κατὰ τὸν Ἰλισσὸν διῆξε φωνὴ βοῶντός του, Σώκρατες, Σώκρατες. ὡς δὲ ἐπιστραφεὶς περιεσκόπουν ὁπόθεν εἴη Κλεινίαν ὁρῶ τὸν Ἀξιόχου θέοντα ἐπὶ Καλλιρρόην.

[2] Herod. VI. 137 αὐτοὶ Ἀθηναῖοι λέγουσι...φοιτᾶν γὰρ ἀεὶ τὰς σφετέρας θυγάτερας ἐπ᾿ ὕδωρ ἐπὶ τὴν Ἐννεάκρουνον.

despots, yet the name *Fair-Fount* was, when Thucydides wrote, evidently a matter of antiquarian knowledge.

The question now before us is, Have we evidence that a spring, naturally small but reinforced and rearranged at the time of the despots, existed in the district enclosed by the Pnyx, Areopagos, and Acropolis? A glance at the plan in Fig. 35 will show that such evidence does indeed exist. In the Pnyx rock at the point marked Y is the spring Kallirrhoë, Fair-Fount. It has been reinforced by water from the district of the Ilissus, brought in the conduit of Peisistratos. In front of the ancient Kallirrhoë once stood a Fountain-House, also of the date of the despots, the Fountain-House called Nine-Spouts, Enneakrounos.

The evidence for this threefold statement must be examined in detail. But first a word must be said as to the geological conditions of the site so far as they bear on the water-supply of Athens.

For her water-supply, and especially for her drinking water, Athens depends, has always depended, not on her rivers but her wells. In describing the Enneakrounos Pausanias[1] says, 'There are wells throughout all the city, but this is the only spring.' His statement as regards the spring is not strictly correct. Besides Kallirrhoë the ancient city possessed two natural springs, and these both on the Acropolis itself, the Klepsydra at the North-West corner and the spring in the precinct of Asklepios on the South slope. About the wells he is right. The plain on which Athens stood was, owing to its geological structure, amply supplied with wells. Its uppermost stratum is of calcareous stone, the material of which the hills of Lykabettos, of the Mouseion, and the Acropolis are all formed. Through this stratum rain can freely filter. But beneath this calcareous layer is a second stratum of slate and marl; this is practically impermeable, and here water collects into wells.

Wells, then, occur sporadically all over Athens and the Athenian plain, but nowhere in such abundance as in the district under discussion[2]. The Pnyx and the Mouseion on the

[1] Paus. I. 14. 1 φρέατα μὲν γὰρ καὶ διὰ πάσης τῆς πόλεώς ἐστι, πηγὴ δὲ αὕτη μόνη.
[2] For what follows I am entirely indebted to Herr Gräber's final investigations, completing those of Prof. Dörpfeld. See 'Enneakrounos,' *A. Mitt.* 1905, p. 58.

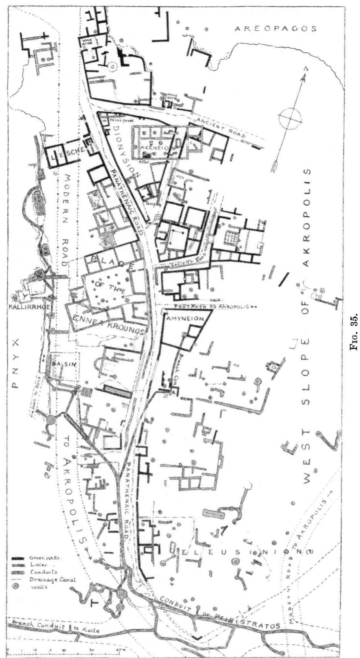

AREOPAGOS

ANCIENT ROAD

DIONYSION

PANATHENAIC ROAD

MODERN ROAD

LESCHE

BACCHEION

PEIRA THINA

PLAC OF THE ENNEA KROUNOS

KALLIRRHOE

PNYX

AMYNEION

FOOT PATH TO AKROPOLIS

BASIN

TO AKROPOLIS

PANATHENAIC ROAD

WEST SLOPE OF AKROPOLIS

ELEUSINION (?)

MODERN ROAD TO AKROPOLIS

CONDUIT OF PEISISTRATOS

Branch Conduit to Koile

Greek walls
Later
Conduits
Drainage Canal
Wells

Fig. 35.

8—2

one side, the Areopagos and Acropolis on the other form, as will readily be seen by reference to Fig. 46, a sort of trough, in which both rain and subterranean water are caught and must necessarily accumulate. As the ground slopes towards the North and the West the water accumulated cannot make its way towards the Ilissos. Its only outlet is the narrow and inadequate passage between the Pnyx and the Areopagos to the Eridanos. It is not surprising that, though the district lies high above the bed of the Eridanos, it was somewhat marshy. That its watery character was early turned to account and led to a dense population is shown by the fact that no less than 100 wells have been sunk within its narrow limits. These wells will be seen dotted about all over the plan in Fig. 35. These wells for subterranean water are frequently reinforced by cisterns for collecting rain-water. The cisterns are easily distinguished from the wells by the fact that they are lined with cement. Sometimes an old well which has presumably run dry has been turned by a coat of cement into a cistern. It is very remarkable that, long before the days of Peisistratos, elaborate systems existed for collecting water, in wells, cisterns, and conduits; one canal extended as far as the Odeion of Herodes Atticus, and followed a course almost coincident with that of Peisistratos, which it long preceded. Its complex of wells is clearly seen at T in Fig. 35, a little to the North of the 'Branch Conduit to Koile.'

It is beside our purpose to examine in detail the artificial water-supply [1] of the district before the time of Peisistratos. That such a system existed is worth noting, because it shows that the district is a good site for the *Limnae*, and also that it was from early days thickly populated.

Our immediate concern, however, is to fix, if possible, the site of Kallirrhoë. Nor is this difficult. As the traveller goes by the modern carriage road from the 'Theseion' to the Acropolis, and as he nears the Pnyx he will see on his right a number of rock-chambers and channels cut in the rock, originally buried out of sight but laid bare by the making of the modern road. These are shown in Fig. 35 to the right and left of the spot marked Kallirrhoë, and appear more plainly on the enlarged plan in

---

[1] Fully discussed by Herr Gräber, *op. cit.*

Fig. 38, where they are marked r¹—r¹⁰.   They are a succession
of rock-hewn wells and cisterns and channels, dating from early
Greek to Roman times.   Their number is additional evidence
that the rock of the Pnyx had a regular system for collecting
water, but of the series two only concern us, those marked
r⁶ and r⁷.

An enlarged plan of the wells r⁶ and r⁷, with their connecting
passages and chambers, is given in Fig. 36.   A detailed description of it is important, because these chambers, recognized as
forming the ancient Kallirrhoë, are now closed to the public by
a locked gate, behind which few visitors to Athens penetrate.

A narrow stairway, a—b, leads into a chamber (Y) hewn in the
heart of the rock.   This chamber is about 4 metres square, and

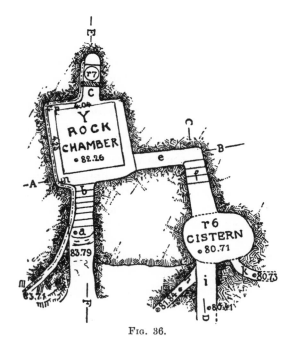

Fig. 36.

has an arched roof.   Immediately opposite the entrance to Y, in
the Western wall, a niche 1·80 m. deep has been cut (C).   In this
niche the shaft of a well (r⁷) has been sunk 2 metres deep.   This

is clearly shown in section in Fig. 43. In front of the well was
a barrier, so that water could be drawn without fear of falling in.
Over the well, about 0·80 metre above the pavement, was a small
niche, which may have held an image. From the entrance of the
chamber Y, about 1·30 metres high from the ground, there is a
channel, n—p, worked in the rock. It has a slight inclination
towards the niche C, and was obviously meant to collect the
water that oozed from the vaulted roof and the walls. Later it
was used as a conduit for the new water-supply brought by
Peisistratos. Remains of a lead pipe and a terra-cotta conduit
were found at m.

For,—doubt is impossible,—we have here in the niche at C the
ancient Kallirrhoë. The large rock chamber Y marks it out from
the other wells. Its importance down to Roman times is shown
by the fact that the chamber Y is paved with a rich mosaic, the
patterns of which are like those made elsewhere in Athens in
the time of Hadrian. The ancient well must have kept its
sanctity, otherwise it would not have been so adorned. After
the well had run dry, and when the water-supply was purely
artificial, the walls and ceiling were carefully cemented and the
cement was later renewed. Such a coating would of course have
been impossible when the roof and walls were dripping with
natural water.

At the right hand of the entrance to Y was a passage, e—f,
leading down by steps into a large elliptical chamber, r⁶. This
chamber, presumably a cistern, was paved in Roman days with
marble slabs, but below the marble pavement is a stucco
pavement of Greek date. From this cistern leads a channel, i,
which may have led to the well-house of Peisistratos, or, as
suggested in the restoration (Fig. 43), to a smaller subordinate
fountain.

The supply of water at Kallirrhoë was slender. We have seen
that efforts were made to reinforce it by well-sinking, by conduits,
by cisterns. But, though the Athenians found the water of
Kallirrhoë adequate for their ritual baths, they had other needs,
and, as the city grew and grew, the effort to cope locally with the
increasing demand proved futile. There was a crying need for
water from a distance, a great popular need such as the despots
loved to supply. Water was needed, and water was brought in

a supply practically inexhaustible, from the district of the upper Ilissos.

By a happy chance in the history of excavations, long before the search for the aqueduct of the despots began, another aqueduct, the work of another despot, had been brought to light—the aqueduct that Polycrates made for the Samians. At the close of his account of Polycrates, Herodotus[1] tells us he had lingered long over the affairs of the Samians 'because they possessed three of the most wonderful works ever accomplished by the Greeks.' The first and the only one of these wonders that concerns us was a great aqueduct bored through a mountain 150 fathoms high. The length of the tunnel, he goes on to say, was seven stadia, the height and the breadth eight feet each way. Through this tunnel there went a second passage, 20 cubits deep by three feet wide, through which the water is carried along in tiled pipes from a great spring to the city of Samos. The architect of this tunnel was a Megarean, Eupalinos, son of Naustrophos.

Possibly, *pace* Herodotus, even if the Samians had had no aqueduct he would anyhow have told us the story of the ring; be that as it may, his account of the first wonder, the aqueduct, is invaluable, and has been fully substantiated. Never was a town by nature worse off for its water-supply than Samos, and rarely has one been supplied by a more astonishing piece of engineering. The 'great spring' Hagniades has been found[2], the tunnel with its double channel, even the very earthenware pipes laid down by Eupalinos. We know perfectly well what to expect in an aqueduct made by the despots.

The excavators naturally sought for the conduit of Peisistratos in the immediate neighbourhood of Kallirrhoë, and there, close up to the Pnyx rock, they found it, at a distance of about 40 metres from the rock chamber Y. From that point up to the South of the Odeion of Herodes Atticus its course has been completely excavated. It is best seen in Professor Dörpfeld's official plan (Fig. 46). Just South of the Odeion the conduit could not be cleared out, because of its damaged condition and the mass of *débris* that had fallen over it. Between the Odeion and the

[1] Herod. III. 60.
[2] For a full account of the Samos aqueduct, see Dr Fabricius, *A. Mitt.* IX. 1884, p. 175.

Dionysiac theatre it runs beneath an ancient road, and passes within the precinct of Dionysos, between the earlier and later temples.   Beyond that point its course has not been excavated in detail, but beneath the modern Russian church a conduit passes which must be its continuation, and this leads on to the watercourse[1] discovered long ago, now utilized for watering the Royal Gardens.   This water is known to come from the upper valley of the Ilissus (Fig. 49).

The main conduit ran, then, from the upper valley of the Ilissus to the great reservoir basin marked on the plan in Fig. 35, but from this main conduit several branches can be traced; the most important are the branch tunnel that leads to the district of Koile and a smaller branch that goes off to water the Amyneion. Other ramifications can be traced, the object of which is not always clear; they probably occur at points where in piercing the tunnel veins of water were reached, and some served to bring to the main conduit subsidiary supplies from the Hill of the Muses and from the Acropolis.

Only those, as Professor Dörpfeld[2] himself remarks, who have taken the trouble to get right down into the tunnellings and cross tunnellings and explore them thoroughly so far as they can be explored, can form any idea of the magnitude of the work. Sometimes it is possible to stand upright in the conduit, some portions can only be reached on the hands and knees.   The fact is borne in upon any one and every one who has made even a brief exploration, he feels himself unquestionably exploring what must have been the main artificial water-supply of ancient Athens, and here, if such a supply were needed, must have been the centre of the ancient city life.

The aqueduct is dated securely by comparison with the work of Eupalinos at Samos as of the time of the despots.   Two striking analogies are observable between the aqueduct of Peisistratos at Athens and that of Polycrates at Samos.   These are the character of the pipes, and the system of shafts.   The separate

---

[1] Examined and discussed by Dr E. Ziller, *A. Mitt.* II. p. 112, and see Herr Gräber, 'Die Enneakrounos,' *A. Mitt.* 1905, p. 58.

[2] The account is taken entirely from the official reports by Prof. Dörpfeld after examination of the site under his guidance.   See Bibliography, *Enneakrounos*, and for the more recent supplementary investigations of Herr Gräber 'Enneakrounos,' *A. Mitt.* 1905, xxx. p. 1.

pieces of the pipes at Athens are from 0·60 m. to 0·61 in length, not counting the junction points. They are made of fine yellowish clay; inside they are protected by a red glaze, outside they are left rough, except that at each end they are glazed and have a double stripe of glaze round the middle and round each end. In length and diameter they correspond with the Samos pipes, which Professor Dörpfeld carefully inspected for comparison[1]. The Samos pipes also are actually decorated with stripes, only the stripes at Samos are incised, those at Athens painted.

The same correspondence is notable in the way the pipes are joined together: both at Athens and Samos the pipes are soldered together with lead, and provision is made at both places for cleaning them. An elliptical shaped hole large enough to admit the hand is left, and is provided with a cover. A specimen of the Athenian pipes is shown in Fig. 37, and side by side with it a section of the conduit with the pipe in position.

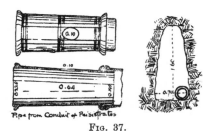

Pipe from Conduit of Peisistratos

Fɪɢ. 37.

The pipes bear abundant traces of long use and frequent repair. In quite early days they seem to have got crusted with lime deposit from the water, and in some cases quite choked up, the water then flowed over the pipes and flooded the main channel to two-thirds of its height. In some places, where the rock was soft, it seems to have got worn away and fallen in, and portions of the tunnel became useless. New borings were made for about 30 metres and new pipes put in; these were quadrangular instead of round, but in the disused portion of the tunnel the old round pipes still lie about.

Secondly, as at Samos, at intervals of from 30 to 40 metres, both tunnels alike are provided with shafts, which served when

[1] *A. Mitt.* xviii. 1893, p. 223.

the tunnels were first made for the clearing away of the rock fragments, and which were made use of for the like purpose when the conduit was excavated. These shafts are sunk perpendicularly; one of them reached down to a depth of 12 metres, so low does the conduit in places lie.

Of cardinal importance to us is the point at which the conduit debouches, because near to that point we may hope to find the fountain-house 'Nine-Spouts.' The conduit ends in an arrangement which is somewhat surprising, and which will be best understood by reference to Fig. 38. To the extreme left, at a point near letter B, the conduit emerges. It here consists of a massive channel built of blocks of *poros* stone, indicated by the thick black lines on the plan. At point a^4 it ends in the Pnyx rock. But, and this is the odd thing, at a^3, about eight metres before the channel ends, a pipe issues from the stone channel and running parallel to the Pnyx rock conducts the water to the main reservoir (Haupt-Bassin). A similar arrangement has been observed in the aqueduct at Samos. There, too, the conduit pipe leaves the rock channel before it ends. It is conjectured[1] that this was a plan intended to mislead an enemy who might desire to cut off the water-supply.

The conduit actually debouches at a^5 into the great reservoir from which the new fountain-house Nine-Spouts must have been fed. Here, at the reservoir, we find indications of three successive structures. First a structure of very early date, possibly of the time of Solon. Second that of Peisistratos. Third a late Roman structure. Of the two earlier structures no masonry remains, but the position and dimensions can roughly be made out by markings on the Pnyx rock, out of which the West side of the basin was hewn. The exact size of the original basin, which was smaller than the later one, cannot now be determined. In the time of Peisistratos it was enlarged and deepened; the floor of the basin was sunk nearly 1·50 metres deeper. The great basin of Peisistratos was lined with masonry, the blocks of which have now disappeared. In Roman days the place of the great basin of Peisistratos was taken by a quite small structure. This change must have taken place before the building of the late

---

[1] By Herr Gräber, *op. cit.* p. 26.

Roman villa which occupied the place where once the 'Nine-Founts' stood.   When the villa was built the great reservoir had for some time been disused, and the water from the aqueduct, not being needed on the spot in any large quantity, was carried by pipes to the lower city to the North for the supply of the new Roman market-place.   These alterations as to water-supply, it should be noted, are of the first importance in questions of topography, and change in the direction or the extension of an aqueduct is naturally the index of a shifting of population.

The restoration by Professor Dörpfeld (Fig. 38) is, it must

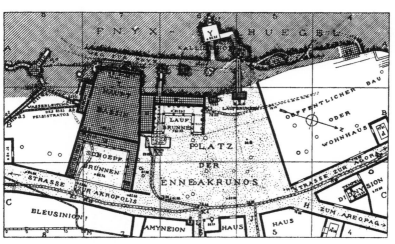

FIG 38.

clearly be understood, to a large extent conjectural.   It must be consulted strictly in conjunction with the plan in Fig. 35, where the actual remains of Greek date are clearly marked in solid black lines.   So used it can be of great service in helping us mentally to reconstruct scattered fragments of masonry that would otherwise be unintelligible.

Some of the details of the restoration have been suggested by the waterworks discovered at Megara, which are in some respects better preserved than those at Athens.   At Megara are extant not only a great conduit to bring water from a distance but an elaborate arrangement for utilizing it consisting of a reservoir and a pillared draw-well besides a fountain house. It is very probable that the works of Theagenes served as a model to Peisistratos, and therefore before the draw-well and fountain house of Peisistratos are discussed a word must be said of the excavations at Megara.

Pausanias[1] begins his account of the city of Megara somewhat abruptly thus. 'In the city there is a fountain. And Theagenes built it for them. About him I have already mentioned that he gave his daughter in marriage to Kylon the Athenian. This Theagenes, having possessed himself of the tyranny, built the

From Fountain of Theagenes Megara.　Athen. Mitth. XXV. 1900 ∤. 30

Waterworn stone from Enneakrounos.

FIG. 39.

fountain, and from its size, its decorations, and the number of its columns, it is worth looking at. Water flows into it called

[1] Paus. I. 40. 1 οὗτος ὁ Θεαγένης τυραννήσας ᾠκοδόμησε τὴν κρήνην μεγέθους ἕνεκα καὶ κόσμου καὶ ἐς τὸ πλῆθος τῶν κιόνων θέας ἀξίαν· καὶ ὕδωρ ἐς αὐτὴν ῥεῖ καλούμενον Σιθνίδων νυμφῶν.

the water of the Sithnidian nymphs.' After the excavations at Athens, the fountain or, as perhaps it is best called, the well-house of Theagenes at Megara was sought and found[1] at the bottom of the Eastern Acropolis of Megara, called Karia. The aqueduct leading to the reservoir was excavated for a considerable distance, and proved to be a structure closely resembling those found at Athens and Samos. Eupalinos it will be remembered was a native of Megara. The draw-well, the supporting walls of which are well preserved, was about 15 by 20 metres in size and built of Kara limestone, a material much used in the 6th century B.C. for the foundations and stylobates of buildings. All round the side whence water was drawn was a low parapet wall. This wall shows signs in many places of being worn away by the friction of ropes and dripping of water. The block shown in Fig. 39 is closely paralleled by the block found in Athens and placed beneath it for comparison.

Not only, then, at Athens did a despot build a well-house and artificially increase a supply of holy water. The original spring at Megara was sacred to the Sithnidian nymphs; we do not know what nymphs guarded Kallirrhoë at Athens; there were plenty about, for to this day close at hand is the Hill of the Nymphs. Dionysos who dwelt so near was called Limnaios, He-of-the-Marshes, Phanodemos[2] says, because he invented the blending of must with water; hence, he adds, 'the springs are called Nymphs and nurses of Dionysos, because water mixed with wine increases it.'

We return to the water-worn stone, the details of which are shown in Fig. 40. This stone is of great architectural importance. From it can be deduced not only the date of the building to which it belonged, but also something of its dimensions and general appearance. The date is fixed by the clamp mark at C. The clamp itself has disappeared, but its shape is proved by the mark of its insertion. Clamps of the ⌐──┐ shape only appear at Athens in buildings of about the date of Peisistratos,

---

[1] Dellbrück and Vollmöller, 'Das Brunnenhaus des Theagenes,' *A. Mitt.* 1900, xxv. p. 23, pl. vii. and viii.

[2] ap. Athen. xi. § 465 ὅθεν καὶ Λιμναῖον κληθῆναι τὸν Διόνυσον, ὅτι μιχθὲν τὸ γλεῦκος τῷ ὕδατι τότε πρῶτον ἐπόθη κεκραμένον. Διόπερ ὀνομασθῆναι τὰς πηγὰς Νύμφας καὶ τιθήνας τοῦ Διονύσου ὅτι τὸν οἶνον αὐξάνει τὸ ὕδωρ κιρνάμενον.

e.g. on the earlier temple of Dionysos Eleuthereus. Our stone
belonged to a building of the date of Peisistratos. As regards

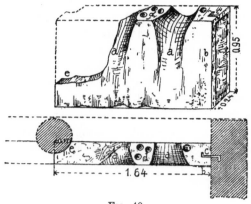

FIG. 40.

the character of the building, it is clear from the curve at e which
is a segment of a circle, that the stone was at this point cut away
to receive a pillar. The unworn condition of the stucco at
b leads Professor Dörpfeld to conclude that the stone was a corner
stone, the angle protecting the stucco from friction. The distance
between these two points, e and b, gives the measurement of the
intercolumniations. From this one stone it is *certain* that a draw-
well of the date of Peisistratos existed and that it was surmounted
by a colonnade. Its appearance must have been somewhat that
of the draw-well (Schoepf-brunnen) restored in Fig. 38. We pass
to the consideration of the fountain house Nine-Spouts.

The great open square marked 'place of the Enneakrounos'
(Fig. 38) is really the site of Nine-Spouts. This is clear from
many considerations. 1. Nine-Spouts must have stood over
or in front of Fair-Fount which it superseded. Over it would
be an impossible situation, because of the Pnyx rock, so we
may securely place it in front. 2. Nine-Founts must have stood
about two metres below the level of the basin, from which it
was fed, in order that the water might flow easily in. 3. At K 2
and K 3 are the beginnings of two ancient subterranean canals
which must have been intended to carry off the superfluous water
from Nine-Spouts. 4. Straight down to this open place comes

the foot-way from the Acropolis and thither also all the rest of
the roads ultimately converge. 5. The place must have been in
Greek times an open place, as no foundations of Greek buildings
have been found, only the remains of a great Roman house, and
under it countless wells.

This Roman house consisted of a large atrium with a peristyle
of twelve columns and several small chambers surrounding it.
The walls are a patchwork of materials of all kinds, and even
the bases of the columns are made up of fragments from other
buildings. One of these fragments belonging to the draw-well
we have already discussed, another, we shall immediately see,
belongs to Nine-Spouts itself.

Can we form any mental picture of Nine-Spouts? Fortunately
vase-paintings come to our aid. It is not a little remarkable that
in the decoration of black-figured water-vases (hydriae) of the

Fig. 41.

6th century B.C., there appears a sudden fashion in fountain-
houses. Of hydriae so decorated the British Museum contains
no less than ten. One of these[1] is reproduced in Fig. 41. The

[1] Brit. Mus. Cat. B. 329, *Antike Denkmäler* II. Taf. 19. On another vase in the
British Museum (Cat. B 331) is inscribed Kalire Krene, Spring Fair-Fount, and on
it also occurs the name *Hippokrates*, which *may* be intended for the brother of
Kleisthenes; see *Myth. and Mon. Anc. Athens*, Fig. 20.

Fountain-House depicted is of the usual shape, a tetrastyle Doric portico. The architectural details are very clear, the triglyphs and guttae standing out in white. In actual architecture they would both be painted blue. Four maidens are water-drawing. Two of them are hanging up wreaths. Over three of them their names are inscribed Iope, Rhodopis, Kleo. But what at once arrests our attention is the arrangement of the water-spouts. Facing us are three, a lion's head and two horsemen, to either side of these is a lion's head spout; that makes not a Nine-Spouts but a Five-Spouts. But, drawn in perspective as they must be, do not the side spouts each represent three? It is at least probable that we have an arrangement like that restored in Fig. 38, three spouts facing, and three at each side. Lion-spouts are of course frequent in Fountain-Houses. The horsemen of our vase are unique; they give the Fountain-House a dashing despotic air.

We know then just what sort of architectural fragments, we might expect to find; we can imagine a fragment that would be conclusive. A 'Doric' portico might belong to more than one kind of building, a lion's head spout could belong only to a Fountain-House. No lion's head has been found, but instead, what is as good for our purpose, *a stone hollowed out for the reception of a lion's head.* This stone is shown in Fig. 42.

Fig. 42.

Not only is the space for the lion's head evident, but behind is clearly visible the hole for the pipe. The block is of blue calcareous stone such as is found both on the Acropolis and the Pnyx. Of exactly the same limestone is a small remnant of

a polygonal wall from the South boundary of the precinct of
the Fountain-House.

The plan in Fig. 38 makes the general disposition of the
place of the Enneakrounos clear, the large reservoir behind
(Haupt-Bassin), immediately in front of it the draw-well (Schoepf-
brunnen), and to the right of the reservoir, and of course equally
fed by it, Nine-Spouts (Lauf-brunnen). In front a great open
space. What is matter for conjecture is the exact site and size of
Nine-Spouts. A clear view of the relation of Nine-Spouts to
Fair-Fount is given in the sectional restoration[1] in Fig. 43. There

FIG. 43.

we see the vaulted rock chamber Y, the actual well, Kallirrhoë, to
which it led, and in front of it, the modern road intervening,
Nine-Spouts or Enneakrounos itself. In front of that again
the open space, possibly once enclosed, was the heart and centre
of the agora.

Before we pass to the question of the agora it may be worth
while to notice that the well-house, Enneakrounos, Nine-Spouts,

[1] Mr F. M. Cornford draws my attention to the striking resemblance between
the plan of the Kallirrhoë cavern (Figs. 36 and 43) and the curious arrangement of the
'cavernous underground chamber' which in Plato (*Rep.* VII. 514) symbolizes the
prison-house of earthly existence. This chamber was entered by a long and steep
descent from the outer air and had at the opposite end a low parapet, answering to
the well-parapet in Kallirrhoë. Even the image in the niche has its Platonic
counterpart in the shadows cast by the fire-light upon the inmost wall from the
images carried along the parapet. One can imagine that Plato himself had often
visited the well, had seen his own shadow thrown across the parapet by the torch
of his guide standing at the foot of the entrance-stair, and heard the echo of his
own voice as though it were proceeding from the shadow (Plat. *Rep.* 515 B).

was known as late as the seventeenth century to have been on the West slope of the Acropolis. In the curious old plan, then drawn by Guillet and Coronelli[1], a portion of which is reproduced in Fig. 44, we have on the West slope not only a well against which in the key to the plan is marked 'Enneakrounos,' but also close to it the ruins of a small theatre, which may well stand for the Odeion as seen by Pausanias. In another plan of the seventeenth century, usually known as the plan of the Capucins, both theatre and Enneakrounos are missing, and in their place stands

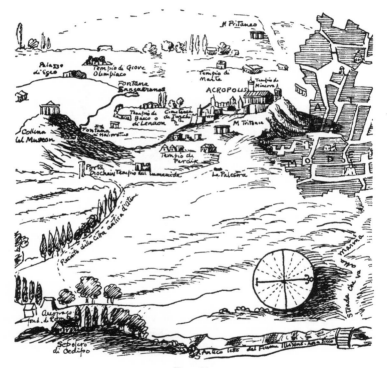

FIG. 44.

the so-called 'Theseion.' On close examination it may be seen that on the Capucin plan, the theatre, the Enneakrounos, and some other buildings have been obliterated and other monuments

[1] Omont, *Athènes au* XVII *siècle*, Pl. XXXIX.

drawn in over them.   It may be taken therefore as certain[1] that, in the seventeenth century, remains of an 'Enneakrounos,' and of a theatre-like building near it, existed.

We have had to reconstruct the *Nine-Spouts* as best we might from the analogy of well-houses on vase-paintings, from the remains of the well-house at Megara, and from a few scattered, though significant stones.   We have also *inferred* its importance from the vast system of water-works of which it was the manifest goal.   But there is another witness to its past greatness.   It is the place where all ways meet.   The irregular square in front of the well-house Nine-Spouts and in part occupied by it was manifestly a great centre of the city life.   The complex of ancient roads is best seen in Fig. 46.   The great Panathenaic way passes along its Eastern side, but that is not all.   The branch roads from the Areopagos converge thither.   Most important of all for us, straight down from the Acropolis gate, skirting the Amyneion, there descends a narrow footway.   By this we may be sure the King's daughters descended to fetch water from Kallirrhoë.

A word must be said as to the nature and surroundings of the main ancient road, which topographically is of capital importance. Somewhere along its course must have lain the ancient Agora. Our first impression is, unexpectedly, of narrowness, just as it is when we stand on the other Sacred Way, at Delphi.   On the Panathenaic way five persons can only just stand abreast; the chariots must have gone in single file.   It is in fact a narrow Oriental street.   It is bounded on either side by walls of good polygonal masonry and is hemmed in, as is seen on the map, by houses and precincts.   Beneath the road is an elaborate system of drainage pipes with shafts by which they could be entered for cleaning purposes.   There are of course many cross-roads, two to the left leading to the Areopagos, one to the Pnyx, another to Koile.   The footway leading straight to the Acropolis has already been noted.

One of the best preserved portions of the road is that which runs along by the Western side of the precinct of *Dionysos-in-the-*

---

[1] See Prof. Dörpfeld, *A. Mitt.* xx. p. 510, 1895.

Marshes. Here the polygonal walls on both sides are well preserved. Almost opposite the wine-press we come on buildings
which, from inscriptions, can be dated as of the sixth and fifth
centuries B.C. These consist of an open exedra, quadrangular
in shape and of polygonal masonry. Inside this precinct is a
small shrine with no columns, in front of it an altar of *poros*
stone. Both material and technique point to the sixth century B.C. To whom the shrine is dedicated is not known.
Thucydides could perhaps have told us. In the course of the
century next following the shrine must have fallen into disuse.
As the level of the road rose it would, once disused, speedily get
covered up. That this was actually the case is clearly shown by
the fact that a building of the fourth century B.C. was super-
imposed. It extended right back to the Pnyx rock. Two boundary
stones of this later building are still[1] *in situ* in the wall bordering
on the main road; on each is inscribed 'Boundary of the Lesche'
(ὅρος λέσχης). Immediately next to the South comes a building
of polygonal limestone masonry. Two inscriptions show that this
building was mortgaged, so it must have been a private house.
Beyond this there is nothing of special interest till we come to
the great open place in which stood the fountain Nine-Spouts.

The careful engineering of the road, its elaborate drainage,
the way it is close packed on either side with houses and sanctuaries leave us no doubt but that in it we have the one and, it
appears, the only chariot-way from the agora to the Acropolis.
The shrines that line this regular approach lie essentially and
emphatically *towards that part of the city.*

So far we have considered the road as an approach, but it
must always be remembered that historically we have to reverse
our procedure. The city grows *from* the central hill, not *towards*
it, and that outward growth is clear. It may be traced on the
map in Fig. 46. The ancient agora lay in the hollow between the
hills directly overlooked by the assembly place on the Pnyx; then
as it outgrew these narrow limits it was forced bit by bit round the
West shoulder of the Areopagus, and there turned Eastward by
the hill Kolonos Agoraios, on which stands the 'Theseion'; below

[1] Prof. Dörpfeld writes to me—'Unhappily this is no longer true; the inscribed
stones have been stolen.'

that hill was the Stoa Basileios, which in the fifth century B.C. was assuredly part of the agora. The agora could not spread Westward; the hill prevented that; it was forced always Eastward, first in Hellenistic days as far as the Stoa of Attalos, then in Roman days to the Gate of the Roman Agora and the Tower of the Winds. Such is its long but simple story. If we follow the water-course of Peisistratos and its later Roman extension we shall not go wrong.

The houses that covered the square in front of Nine-Spouts, and into which fragments of the well-house were built, are all of Roman date. Clear them away, and we have, as has been seen, a great quadrangular space in front of the city well, a place to which all ways converge (Fig. 46). Surely here, if anywhere, is the ancient agora, close to the city gates.

It is remarkable that, visiting Athens half a century before the excavations began, an English scholar, Christopher Wordsworth[1], by sheer light of common sense, saw that here, and here only, could the ancient agora be, and here he marked it on his quaint, rudimentary map (Fig. 45). His words are, as contrasted with later confusions, memorable. ' In order,' he says, ' to obtain a distinct notion of the natural characteristics of the spot to which we refer, let us consider it in the *first place* as abstracted from all artificial modifications; let us imagine ourselves as existing in the days of Kekrops, and looking upon the site of Athens. In a wide plain, which is enclosed by mountains except on the South, where it is bounded by the sea, rises a flat, oblong rock lying from East to West about fifty yards high, rather more than one hundred and sixty broad, and about three hundred in length. It is inaccessible on all sides but the West, on which it is approached by a steep slope. This the future Acropolis or Citadel of Athens. We place ourselves upon this eminence and cast our eyes about us. Immediately on the West is a second hill, of irregular form, lower than that on which we stand and opposite to us. This is the Areopagus. Beneath it on the South-West is a valley neither deep nor narrow, open both at the North-West and South-East. Here was the Agora or public place of Athens. Above it to the South-West rises another hill, formed like the

[1] Wordsworth, *Greece pictorial, descriptive and historical*, p. 133, 1839.

two others already mentioned of hard and rugged limestone, clothed here and there with a scanty covering of herbage. On this hill the popular assemblies of the future citizens of Athens will be held. It will be called the Pnyx. To the South of it is a fourth hill, of similar kind, known in after-ages as the Museum.

Fig. 45.

Thus a group of four hills is presented to our view, which nearly enclose the space wherein the Athenian Agora existed, as the Forum of Rome lay between the hills of the Capitol and the Palatine.'

The secret of Dr Wordsworth's insight lies in the words, 'we place ourselves upon the eminence and cast our eyes about us.' He stood on the actual hill, realized, as Thucydides did, that that was the beginning of things, noted the shape of the hill and its only possible approach, and saw that the developments of the city must lie that way, *towards that part*, as Thucydides would say. Half a century later Prof. Dörpfeld, coming with the trained eye of the engineer and architect, made, quite independently of Dr Wordsworth, the same observation. The valley enclosed by the Acropolis, Areopagus, Pnyx, and Mouseion, was then utterly

barren of visible remains; other archaeologists had placed their
agora where ancient remains were visible, North or South of the
Acropolis; Prof. Dörpfeld, in defiance of orthodox tradition, placed
it West, and there his excavations, as we have seen, brought to
light the sanctuary of Dionysos-in-the-Marshes, the ' Nine-Spouts,'
the Panathenaic Way, and the host of sanctuaries, houses, wine-
presses, wells, and water-courses that encompassed the ancient
agora.

Later we shall have to examine what it was that led other scholars
and archaeologists astray; for the present we must return to
Thucydides. He never mentions the agora, his thoughts never
for a moment stray from his city before Theseus. He has shown
its meagre extent and the immediate proximity of its most ancient
sanctuaries, and to clinch his argument he returns to the citadel
itself and its ancient name; he resumes the whole argument (see
p. 8) in its last and most emphatic clause.

Because of the ancient settlement here, the citadel as well (as the
present city) *is still to this day called the city.*

Thucydides is strictly correct both as regards official and
literary usage. An examination of official inscriptions shows
that down to the Peace of Antalcidas (387–6 B.C.) the Acropolis
was officially known as *polis*[1]. The new form 'in the Acropolis' first
appears in the year of the peace[2], and from then on is in regular
use. In literature, both in prose and verse, *polis* is still uniformly
used after a local preposition, *e.g.* towards the *polis*, in the *polis*;
but when there is no local preposition the word acropolis is
employed. Thus, in the *Knights* of Aristophanes[3], when the
Sausage-Seller sees the Goddess herself coming from the *polis*
with her owl perched on her, and there is no shadow of doubt that
Athena is coming from the Acropolis; but Lysistrata[4] says, ' to-day
we shall seize the Acropolis,' where there is no local preposition,
though the sense would have been clear with *polis*. As Dr Wyse[5]
has pointed out, it was easy for the word *polis* to go on being

[1] *C.I.A.* II. 11 and IV. 211 *b*.
[2] *C.I.A.* II. 14. See Foucart, *Bull. de Corr. Hell.* p. 166, 1888.
[3] Ar. *Eq.* 1092   καὶ μοὐδόκει ἡ θεὸς αὐτὴ
        ἐκ πόλεως ἐλθεῖν καὶ γλαῦξ αὐτῇ 'πικαθῆσθαι.
[4] Ar. *Lys.* 175.
[5] *Speeches of Isaeus*, p. 476, where the use of *polis* for *acropolis* is fully discussed.

used for the Acropolis, because the Athenians had another word (ἄστυ), which they used in such phrases as 'in town,' 'to town.'

We have learnt from Thucydides all he has to tell us, and in the light of recent excavations he seems to have spoken clearly enough. The limits of his ancient city have been confirmed by the discovery of the old Pelasgic fortifications. We have seen with our own eyes two of the ancient sanctuaries which lay *towards* his city, the Pythion and the sanctuary of Dionysos-in-the-Marshes; and from literary evidence inferred the two others, the Olympieion and the sanctuary of Ge. We have noted that, in the order in which Thucydides names them, they occur in succession from East to West; and, most convincing of all, near to the last-named sanctuary we have found Nine-Spouts, and not only Nine-Spouts, but the old Fair-Fount that was before it. Thus all seems clear and simple; Thucydides, Pausanias, and modern excavations tell the same harmonious tale.

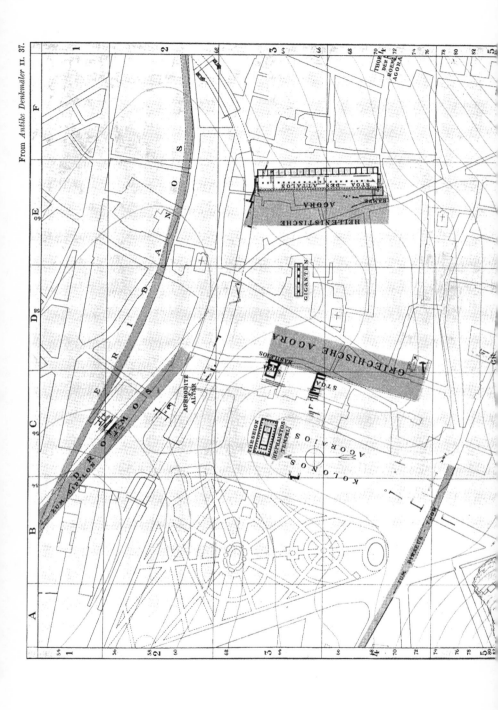

From *Antike Denkmäler* II. 37.

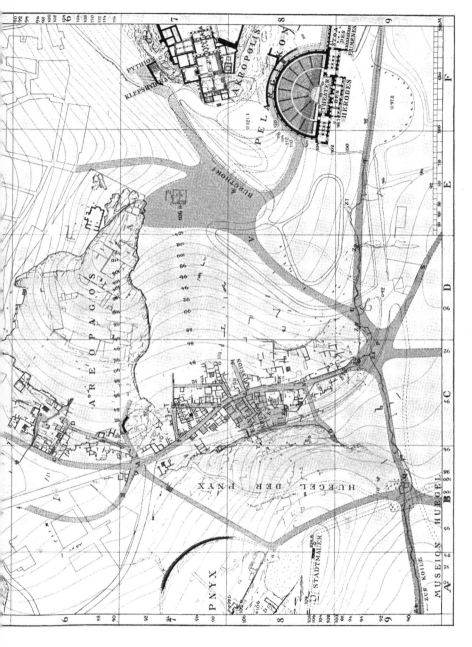

Fig. 46.

CONCLUSION.

HAVING now stated what we believe to be the truth respecting the ancient burgh of Athens, its nature and limits and the position of its early Sanctuaries, we have still, in accordance with the plan proposed at the outset (p. 4), to examine other and, as we believe, erroneous views. These views are widely current in manuals and guide-books and are supported by names[1] that command respect. A study of the genesis of errors so wide-spread and deep-rooted may not be unprofitable.

The sources of error seem to us fourfold, as follows:

1. *The lie of the modern town.*
2. *A misunderstanding of the text of Thucydides.*
3. *The duplication of certain sanctuaries*

and, closely connected with this,

4. *Confusion as to Kallirrhoë and Enneakrounos.*

1. *The lie of the modern town.*

A glance at the map of modern Athens will show that its centre of gravity lies not West but North of the Acropolis—the modern market lies there with its throng of narrow streets and the whole modern town, with its shops, hotels, stations, spreads out in that direction. Moreover, it is obvious that the business part of Roman Athens also lay North. To the North lies the Gate of the Roman agora[2], besides such buildings as the Tower of the Winds and Hadrian's Library (Fig. 49). More than this, the agora of Hellenistic days (Fig. 46) lay there also, and was almost certainly bounded on its Eastern side by the Stoa of Attalos, of which there are

---

[1] See Bibliography.

[2] The map in Fig. 46 is reproduced by Prof. Dörpfeld's kind permission from his official plan published in the *Antike Denkmäler* (II. 37). To discuss the later Greek, Hellenistic and Roman agoras is no part of the object of the present book, but it was thought well to reproduce the plan as showing how the agora spread gradually to the North and also as elucidating the complex of roads that meet at the Enneakrounos.

still substantial remains[1].   Quite recently the foundations of two
other colonnades have come to light[2], just below and to the East
of the hill on which stands the so-called 'Theseion.'   These two
colonnades stand just at the entrance of the Greek agora; the
Northern one is probably either the Basileion or the Stoa
Basileios, the first building described by Pausanias on his entry
into the Kerameikos. .The two last colonnades played no part
in attempted reconstructions of the agora, for the simple reason

FIG. 47.

that they were below ground; but the Stoa of Attalos, that of
the Giants, and the Gateway of the Roman agora have been
regularly regarded as *data* with which any theorist was bound to
start; they had to be fitted in somehow.

---

[1] For the details of this and the other buildings both of the Hellenistic and
Roman agoras, see my *Myth. and Mon. Anc. Athens*, pp. 17—22, 199, 183—203.
[2] *A. Mitt.* 1896, xxi. p. 108.

The next question was, where was the road that led from the agora to the Acropolis, the Panathenaic way ? Given an agora to the North and North-East of the Areopagus, and, given that you were working at home in your study with a flat plan before you, the answer seemed obvious ; the road must have passed straight from the agora round the Eastern end of the Areopagus, and so straight up to the entrance at the Propylaea. The result is a reconstruction of agora and road, like that seen in Fig. 47, a restoration made by Prof. Curtius. So utterly is the West slope of the Acropolis ignored, that it is simply cut off as irrelevant.

Professor Dörpfeld was the first to point out that at the Eastern end of the Areopagus, though there is a footway up to the Acropolis, there is not now a carriage-road, there never was, and, unless the whole natural features of the place are altered, there never will be. The hill at that point, though short, is impracticably steep. What looks easy and obvious on paper is in actuality impossible. Long before he began his excavations Prof. Dörpfeld, with the trained eye of the practical engineer, saw the ancient carriage-way must have followed the modern road, that is, round the West end of the Areopagus between that hill and the Pnyx. From that point by successive windings, then and now, it could climb the hill. The old road we have seen has now been found; it lies in places actually under the new and follows the same course, as natural in 500 B.C. as in 1900 A.D.

One school of topographers, headed by the great name of Curtius, placed the agora at the North side of the Acropolis. We have seen that, though wrong for the beginning of things, this is right for the end. Another school, though they knew that the Roman market lay Northwards, yet had compunctions about the earlier agora. This earlier agora they placed due South of the Acropolis, completely separated from the Roman one. The separation was in idea as well as in place. The early agora was supposed to be in some obscure way a religious, the later a political and commercial centre. Such an arrangement is shown in the plan in Fig. 48[1]. It is purely theoretical and

[1] After the restoration of W. Judeich, *Jahrbuch f. Phil.* CXLI. p. 746. The plan is only given here to illustrate bygone conceptions. I am rejoiced to see that Dr Judeich in his recent *Topographie von Athen*, 1905, accepts the main outlines of Prof. Dörpfeld's topography. See his Plan I.

impossible. The Panathenaic way is made to run North of the Areopagus up the impracticable hill, and the ancient agora lies as a sort of desert island by itself, away from the Council House, the

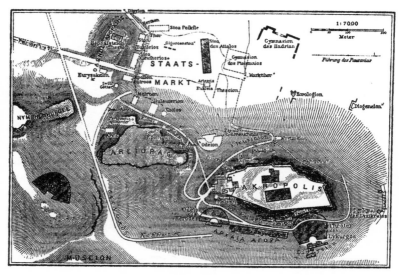

Fig. 48.

Tholos, the Stoa Basileios, and the rest. The West slope is left void. When and how the mysterious leap from old to new, from South to North, was taken no one explained. This brings us to our second source of error.

2. *A misunderstanding of the text of Thucydides.*

What has led topographers to make this singular and un-meaning division of old and new? why have they placed the old agora South of the Acropolis? Simply because, misunderstanding the words of Thucydides, they think *he* placed it South. Thucydides says, it will be remembered (p. 7), that, in the days before Theseus, '*what is now the citadel was the city, together with what is below it towards about South.*' We have seen that the simple and satisfactory expla-nation of the words is that the reference is to the bit of ground known as the Pelargikon, extending mainly West and South-West of the Acropolis and included in the ancient city. We have also seen—and this is of paramount importance—that the sole gist and point of Thucydides' argument is to show the smallness of the ancient city, to prove that it was practically the same as the citadel, only there was this bit over '*towards about South.*' It is the fatal accuracy of Thucydides that has led to his being misunderstood. It is actually thought that he desires to prove *two* points: first, that the ancient city was the citadel; second, that the portion of the city not contained in the citadel was to the South[1]; whereas, as already seen, the *direction* of the city has nothing, could have nothing, to do with the case.

Once embarked on the wrong hypothesis that Thucydides lays two propositions before us, and that one of them is that the city lay to the South, the downward road is easy. The four sanctuaries of Thucydides are selected, it is supposed, to prove the second proposition, i.e. that the city is to the South. Four sanctuaries lie ready, only too ready, to hand. We have, South-East of the Acropolis (Fig. 49), a great Olympieion; we know from Pausanias[2] that close by it was a great Pythion, within the Olympieion was a precinct of Ge; and last and most convincing of all, on the South-East slope of the Acropolis is the great Dionysiac theatre, with its precinct and two temples. Truly a little archaeology is a dangerous thing. So obvious, so striking are these identifications, that at the first glance they seem to compel adhesion.

But a moment's thought obliges us to see that, if tempting, these identifications are impossible. From its *position* the sanctuary of Dionysos Eleuthereus might well have been one of those named by Thucydides, because, as already noted (p. 67), while from his words it would be impossible definitely to say whether the sanctuaries are North, South, East, or West, assuredly the theatre and precinct of Dionysos Eleuthereus *are* 'towards' (πρὸς) the ancient city. But, as we have already (p. 83) seen, it is from this familiar precinct, the sanctuary of the later Dionysos Eleuthereus, that Thucydides is expressly differentiating his more ancient precinct; the same is the case with the Olympieion. Thucydides and everyone at Athens knew that this vast temple

---

[1] For a full statement of this view see Dr Frazer, *Pausanias*, Vol. v. p. 484, and Prof. Ernest Gardner, *Ancient Athens*, p. 141. I regret to see that Prof. Ernest Gardner translates καὶ τὸ ὑπ' αὐτὴν πρὸς νότον μάλιστα τετραμμένον 'and the district *outside it* to the Southward.'

[2] Paus. i. 18. 6 and 7, and i. 19. 1.

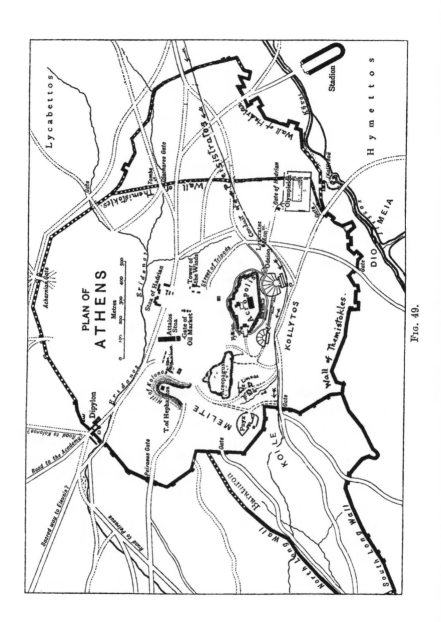

Fig. 49.

was begun in the time of Peisistratos; was it likely to be chosen as a sanctuary to show the limits (or even the direction) of the city of Kekrops?

As regards the Python, special stress has been laid on the fact that it—not the sanctuary on the Long Rocks—is called by Pausanias the Python; but the explanation is easy and manifest; Pausanias is distinguishing it from the other sanctuary of Apollo near at hand, the Delphinion[1].

Sanctuaries so late as these could not fairly be used to prove even the *direction* of the city of Kekrops; but, as already shown, it is not direction, but *size* with which Thucydides is concerned. To give sanctuaries like the Olympieion and Python, which lay outside even the city of Themistocles, as evidence of the small-ness of an ancient 'Mycenaean' city, a Pelasgic fortress, is an absurdity so manifest that statement is refutation. We are brought face to face with the third source of error.

3. *The duplication of certain sanctuaries.*

The misinterpretation of Thucydides has been helped and indeed in a large measure caused by a most curious historical fact, calculated until it was properly understood to mislead any-one. *There was a duplication in two different districts of certain of the most notable Athenian sanctuaries.* To the North and West of the Acropolis, as we have seen in detail, there were sanctuaries of Zeus Olympios, of Apollo Pythios, of Ge and of Dionysos, and near to them was a spring Kallirrhoë, and it is of these, if our view be correct, that Thucydides makes mention, but none the less the fact is patent to everyone who reads Pausanias and visits modern Athens, that to the South-East of the Acropolis there *are* sanctuaries of the same divinities, of Zeus Olympios, of Apollo Pythios, of Ge and of Dionysos, and that near these also is a spring called to this day Kallirrhoë. How did this come to be? What does it signify? The answer once stated[1] is simple and convincing. The duplication of sanctuaries is due to a shift of population from North-West to South-East, from the district of

---

[1] Paus. i. 19. 1. For a full account of this Olympieion and Python which, save for the mistaken identification, do not concern us here, see my *Myth. and Mon. of Anc. Athens*, p. 184.

the Pnyx to the district of the Ilissus. This shift of population is a fact historically attested.

Plutarch[1] in his treatise 'On Banishment' is trying to persuade us that exile is in itself no hardship. He asks, 'Are then those Athenians to be accounted strangers and outlaws who moved from Melite to Diomeia, whence they called the month Metageitnion, and the sacrifice they offered took its name *Metageitnia* from this removal, since they accepted pleasantly and cheerfully their neighbourhood to new people? Surely they are not.' Plutarch's argument does not come to much, but we are grateful to him for recording the fact that there was this shift of population, when or why, alas! we do not certainly know, from Melite in the North-West to Diomeia in the South-East (Fig. 49). Did not the people when they moved take with them their old place-names, their old local legends, their Kallirrhoë? We have curious incidental evidence that they did.

Let us look for a moment at the position of the two demes. As to the position of Melite there has never been any doubt, though its exact boundaries are not clearly defined. Melite was the deme-name given to the hill district West and North-West of the Acropolis. It extended on the West to the barathron, near which cheerful site Themistocles had his home. There, Plutarch[2] tells us, *in Melite*, he built the sanctuary of Artemis Aristoboule which gave such umbrage to the Athenians. Melite was, we know, near the agora and on higher ground. In the opening of the *Parmenides*[3] Kephalos meets Adeimantos in the agora. They want to see Antiphon, and Adeimantos says it will be easy enough for Antiphon has just gone home and 'he lives close by in Melite.' Demosthenes[4] in the speech against Konon says that he was walking in the agora near the Leokorion when he met Ktesias, and Ktesias 'passed on to Melite up hill.'

---

[1] Plut. *de Exil.* VI. ἆρα οὖν ξένοι καὶ ἀπόλιδες εἰσὶν Ἀθηναίων οἱ μεταστάντες ἐκ Μελίτης εἰς Διωμίδα ὅπου καὶ μῆνα Μεταγειτνιῶνα καὶ θυσίαν ἐπώνυμον ἄγουσι τοῦ μετοικισμοῦ τὰ Μεταγείτνια, τὴν πρὸς ἑτέρους γειτνιάσιν εὐκόλως καὶ ἱλαρῶς ἐκδεχόμενοι καὶ στέργοντες; οὐκ ἂν εἴποις. Attention was first drawn to the importance of this passage by Prof. Dörpfeld.
[2] Plut. *Vit. Them.* 22 πλησίον δὲ τῆς οἰκίας κατεσκεύασεν ἐν Μελίτῃ τὸ ἱερόν οὗ νῦν τὰ σώματα τῶν θανατουμένων....
[3] Plat. *Parmenid.* 126 c.
[4] Dem. LIV. 7...παρῆλθε πρὸς Μελίτην ἄνω.

Finally, and for our purpose most important of all, Melite certainly included the Pnyx hill. When Meton appears in the *Birds*[1] and is asked who he is, and where he comes from, he answers

'Meton am I, Greece knows me and Kolonos.'

The scholiast is concerned as to whether it could correctly be stated that Meton was of the deme Kolonos, and *apropos* of this, as to where a certain astronomical monument to Meton had been erected. According to one authority there was a sun-dial in the Pnyx in his memory. The scholiast then adds, 'Is not, some say, *the whole of the district in which the Pnyx is included, the Kolonos called μίσθιος*? So customary has it become to call the part behind the Long Stoa, Kolonos, though it is not. *For all that part is Melite*, and it is so described in the boundaries of the city.' The scholiast is, of course, primarily concerned with the name of the hill dominating the later agora, and on which stands the so-called Theseion (Fig. 46), but incidentally he tells that the deme Melite which included that hill included also the Pnyx. Both points, it will later be seen, are for us important.

Melite then is to the North-West and West of the Acropolis. Where is Diomeia? Its dimensions again are not exactly known, but happily its *direction* is certain (Fig. 49)[2].

In the deme of Diomeia was a gymnasium and a sanctuary of Herakles, both known as *Kynosarges*, and from Herodotus[3] we know in what direction this Kynosarges lay. After Marathon the Persian fleet rounded Sunium with a view to landing at Phalerum, then the port of Athens. Phalerum, of course, lies almost due

---

[1] Ar. *Av.* 999   ἐγὼ Μέτων,
ὃν οἶδεν ῞Ελλας χὠ Κολωνός,

Schol....ἐπὶ ᾽Αψεύδους δὲ τοῦ Πυθοδώρου ἡλιοτρόπιον ἐν τῇ νῦν οὔσῃ ἐκκλησίᾳ πρὸς τῷ τείχει τῷ ἐν τῇ πνυκί. μήποτε οὖν τὸ χωρίον φασί τινες ἐκεῖνο ἅπαν ᾧ περιλαμβάνεται καὶ ἡ Πνύξ, Κολωνός ἐστιν ὁ ἕτερος, ὁ μίσθιος λεγόμενος· οὕτως μέρος τι νῦν σύνηθες γέγονε τὶ Κολωνὸν καλεῖν τὸ ὄπισθεν τῆς μακρᾶς στοᾶς· ἀλλ᾽ οὐκ ἐστι. Μελίτη γὰρ ἅπαν ἐκεῖνο ὡς ἐν τοῖς ὁρισμοῖς γέγραπται τῆς πόλεως.

The mss. have ἐκεῖνο ἐπάνω, Forchammer ἐπάνω ᾧ, Wachsmuth ἅπαν ᾧ, Dobree πᾶν ᾧ. I follow Wachsmuth.

[2] Diomeia is marked on my map (Fig. 49) to the South-East of the Olympieion. My map was drawn before the appearance of Dr Judeich's *Topographie von Athen*; I am glad to see that he (*Topographie*, pp. 155, 158) accepts the position assigned by Professor Dörpfeld to Diomeia. The British School of Archaeology claims to have found the gymnasium of Kynosarges (*Annual of the British School*, 1896—7, p. 89), but as the plans are not yet published I prefer to base my argument on literary evidence.

[3] Herod. vi. 116.

H.   10

South of Athens. The Athenians hurry back from Marathon with all speed to protect the city. They leave the Herakleion at Marathon where they had encamped, and 'take up their station in another Herakleion, that in Kynosarges'—Kynosarges, and with it Diomeia, must therefore lie in or command the direct road between Phalerum and Athens. Pausanias[1] visited Kynosarges and referred to the story of 'the white dog' immediately after the low-lying district of the 'Gardens' on the Ilissus before he visited the stadium.

The Herakleion of Kynosarges has shown us the direction in which Diomeia lay. Diomeia, we have seen, was colonized from Melite. We naturally ask, Was the Herakleion one of the duplicate sanctuaries? In other words, Was there a worship of Herakles in Melite?

In the *Frogs*—a play be it remembered performed at the Lenaia, a festival held originally (p. 88) in the Limnae just below the hill district of Melite—Xanthias is dressing up as Herakles; he says to Dionysos, as he is putting on the lion-skin,

> 'Now watch if Xanthias-Herakles turns faint,
> Or shows the same presence of mind as you';

and Dionysos answers

> 'The real old jail-bird, him from Melite.'

The careful scholiast[2] notes it was not usual to speak of a god as 'from' a place. The Melitean Herakles would normally be described as Herakles 'in' or 'at Melite'; it was treating Herakles as a mere mortal to say Herakles from Melite. But does not the 'from' possibly mark an added joke? Are not the baggage and the donkey and the 'from' all put in to parody the real 'flitting' of Herakles from Melite to Diomeia? That flitting was already accomplished in the time of Aristophanes, for, later on in the play[3], when Aeacus is beating Xanthias-Herakles, and Xanthias

---

[1] Paus. I. 19. 3. Those who following Curtius (*Stadtgeschichte von Athen*, pl. IV.) place Diomeia and Kynosarges North-West on the slopes of Lykabettos have to make Pausanias retrace his steps to visit the stadium.

[2] Schol. *ad* Ar. *Ran.* 501...οὐκ Μελίτης μαστιγίας, σύνηθές τε οὐχ οὕτω λέγειν ἐπὶ θεῶν, οὐκ Μελίτης ἀλλ᾽ ὁ ἐν Μελίτῃ, ὡς καὶ Ζεὺς ὁ ἐν Ὀλυμπίᾳ· ἐπὶ δὲ ἀνθρώπων ἐκ Μελίτης....My attention was drawn to the scholiast's remark in relation to the 'flitting' by Mr Gilbert Murray.

[3] Ar. *Ran.* 650   ἀλλ᾽ ἐφρόντισα
ὁπόθ᾽ Ἡράκλεια τὰν Διομείοις γίγνεται.

utters an involuntary 'whe-ew,' Aeacus asks if he is hurt, and Xanthias recovering himself says,

> 'No ; I was just thinking,
> When my Diomean Feast would next be due.'

The same curious duplication of sanctuaries meets us in the accounts of the initiation of Herakles. The scholiast on the *Frogs*[1] says, 'Herakles was initiated in the Lesser Mysteries in Melite, a deme of Attica,' but by common consent[2] these Lesser Mysteries are held to have taken place at Agrae on the Ilissos, and it is there, according to Stephen[3] of Byzantium, that Herakles obtained initiation. In Melite on or close to the Pnyx hill Pausanias[4] saw beyond the spring 'temples, one built for Demeter and Kore, the other containing an image of Triptolemos.' Did the emigrants from Melite carry their cult down with them to the mystic banks of the Ilissos[5], to Agrae 'where,' according to Eustathius[6], they say 'the Lesser Mysteries of Demeter which they call "those in Agrae" are celebrated'?

Tradition, then, as to the initiation of Herakles was two-fold ; he was initiated in Melite, he was initiated on the banks of the Ilissos at Agrae in Diomeia. We naturally ask, 'Why was he initiated at all, and why did his initiation attract so much attention?' If he was a god it was superfluous, if a pious mortal merely normal. The answer to this question may give a clue to the cause of the shift of population from Melite to Diomeia.

Herakles was initiated because he was an immigrant stranger. We have seen (pp. 27 and 65) that in the 6th century B.C. he was at home on the Acropolis itself; he appears on archaic pediments contending with Triton and the Hydra and on vase-paintings his popularity precedes that of his rival Theseus. Yet, none the

---

[1] Ar. *Ran.* 501 Schol....ἐν γὰρ Μελίτῃ δήμῳ τῆς Ἀττικῆς ἐμυήθη Ἡρακλῆς τὰ μικρὰ μυστήρια.
[2] Plut. *Demetr.* 26. Kleidemos, ap. Bekk. *Anec.* p. 326 Ἄγραι χωρίον ἔξω τῆς πόλεως Ἀθηνῶν, οὗ τὰ μικρὰ τῆς Δήμητρος ἄγεται μυστήρια.
[3] Steph. Byz. Ἄγρα καὶ Ἄγραι χωρίον...ἐν ᾧ τὰ μικρὰ μυστήρια ἐπιτελεῖται μίμημα τῶν περὶ τὸν Διόνυσον, ἐν ᾧ λέγουσι καὶ τὸν Ἡρακλέα μεμυῆσθαι (codd. μεμνῆσθαι).
[4] Paus. I. 14. 2.   [5] Kleidemos, *loc. cit.* παρ' Ἰλισσοῦ μυστικαῖς ὄχθαις.
[6] Eustath. 361. 38 ἀπὸ χώρας πρὸς τῷ Ἰλισσῷ ᾧ κλῆσις Ἄγραι καὶ Ἄγρα, οὗ τὰ μικρὰ τῆς Δήμητρος ἤγετό φησι μυστήρια ἃ ἐλέγετο τὰ ἐν Ἄγραις. Professor Tucker is I believe right in his conjecture (*Class. Rev.* 1904, p. 416) that the Mysteries in the *Frogs* are these Lesser Mysteries and this, as I have pointed out in connection with his discussion (*op. cit.*, p. 418), adds fresh significance to the figure of Herakles.

less, he is a stranger, and his formal reception as a guest was at various places in Attica matter of old world tradition. In the *Lysis* Ktesippos complains that the boys' lovers make for him the weary old boast, that to an ancestor of his belonged the honour of the 'reception of Herakles[1].' Lysis belonged to Aixone, a deme near Phalerum; and by way of the sea in all probability Herakles had come to Athens. Orators, specially religious orators, are less contemptuous. The initiation of Herakles was a telling argument in the mouth of the cosmopolitan peace-loving politician. The Torch-bearer, Kallias[2], in his speech to the Lacedaemonian allies urges the familiar precedent. ' It was right,' he says, ' for us not to bear arms against each other since tradition says, your leader Herakles, and your citizens, the Dioscuri, were the first strangers to whom our ancestor Triptolemos showed the unutterable rites of Demeter and Kore.' Plutarch[3], again, in his *Life of Theseus* tells how the Tyndaridae supported their claim to initiation by citing the analogous case of Herakles. In order to be initiated, Herakles, as a stranger, had to be adopted by a citizen called Pylios; the Tyndaridae, whose exploits were supposed to have taken place at Aphidna, were adopted by Aphidnus. The scene of the initiation of Herakles and the Dioscuri occurs on more than one late red-figured vase[4].

The emphasis laid on the initiation of Herakles and the tradition that he was admitted at the Lesser Mysteries mark the fact that he was a stranger. It is possible to go a step further. Herakles was not merely no true-born Athenian citizen, but an actual foreigner, an Oriental. It is therefore no surprise to us to learn from the best of authorities on Athenian ritual, Apollodorus[5], that ' sacrifice was offered to Herakles Alexikakos at Athens after a special and peculiar manner.' It would be out of place

---

[1] Plat. *Lys.* 205 c ‘Ηρακλέους ξενισμόν.
[2] Xen. *Hell.* vi. 3. 6.   [3] Plut. *Vit. Thes.* 33.
[4] See my *Myth. and Mon. Anc. Athens*, p. 155, Fig. 33.
[5] Apollod. ap. Zenob. *Cant.* v. 22 μῆλον (l. μήλων) ‘Ηρακλῆς. ’Απολλόδωρος ἐν τοῖς περὶ θεῶν ὅτι θύεται ’Αθήνῃσι ‘Ηρακλεῖ ἀλεξικάκῳ ἰδιάζουσά τις θυσιά. Pollux (*Onom.* I. 30) gives the aetiological myth and adds the important detail that the same cultus title *Melon* and the same ritual was in use in Boeotia. καὶ καλεῖται παρὰ τοῖς Θηβαίοις ἢ τοῖς Βοιωτοῖς Μήλων ὁ ‘Ηρακλῆς, ὄνομα ἐκ τοῦ τρόπου τῆς θυσίας λαβών. Melos and Belos appear to be interchangeable forms (Steph. Byz. Βῆλος, ἢ καὶ Μῆλος πρὸς ταῖς ‘Ηρακλέους στήλαις), and of the island Melos we know from the same writer (s.v. Μῆλος) that its earlier colonists were Phenicians, Φοίνικες οὖν οἰκισταὶ πρότερον. Cf. Herakles at Gades, Appian (ed. Bekk. p. 49) says Θρησκεύεται νῦν ἔτι φοινικικῶς.

here to enter upon any detailed examination of the Oriental
elements in the worship of Herakles generally, but as regards his
worship at Athens, and especially in Melite[1], some points must be
noted.

Melite, all authorities seem to agree, is *Malta*[2], the place of
refuge. Diodorus[3] gives us a full description of the original
Melite-Malta and emphasizes, if emphasis were needed, its
harbourage and generally its maritime convenience, its wealth in
arts and crafts and manufactures. 'This island is a colony of the
Phenicians, it lay in mid-ocean and had good harbour, hence
when they extended their trade to the western Ocean it served
them as a refuge.' Of another island of refuge called Melite
Strabo[4] tells us 'the Korybantes removed to Samothrace which was
formerly called Melite.' This Samothrace, according to Diodorus[5],
was called in ancient days *Saonnesos*, Safe-island, which of course
is merely a translation of its Semitic name. In this *Saonnesos-
Melite* the inhabitants down to the time of Diodorus still in *their
sacrificial ceremonies* used many words of a dialect peculiar to
them and, according to tradition, the island got its name in
connection with the story—always a Semitic note—of the Flood.
The inhabitants set up all round the island boundary stones ' of
salvation.'

In the light of *Melite*, 'Refuge,' we begin to understand why
Herakles was worshipped there under the special cultus title of
Alexikakos, 'Preserver-from-Evil[6].' He is Alexikakos, not merely
as the hero of the Labours but by divine right; *as a god* even if

---

[1] The Oriental character of the Herakles cult at Melite was first, I believe,
pointed out by Curtius, and further emphasized by Wachsmuth, *Stadt Athen*,
p. 404 ff. It has never, I believe, been discussed in relation to the shift of population
from Melite to Diomeia.

[2] See Lewy, *Die Semitischen Fremdwörter im Griechischen*, p. 209, the root mālaṭ
מלט to save, מְלִיטָה.

[3] Diod. v. 12 καὶ πρώτη μέν ἐστιν ἡ προσαγορευομένη Μελίτη...ἐστὶ δὲ ἡ νῆσος αὕτη
Φοινίκων ἄποικος οἳ ταῖς ἐμπορίαις διατείνοντες μέχρι τοῦ κατὰ τὴν δύσιν Ὠκεανοῦ καταφυγὴν
εἶχον ταύτην, εὐλίμενον οὖσαν καὶ κειμένην πελαγίαν.

[4] Strab. x. 472...ἀπελθεῖν τούτους (τοὺς Κορύβαντας) εἰς Σαμοθράκην καλουμένην
πρότερον Μελίτην.

[5] Diod. v. 47 ἔνιοι δέ φασι τὸ παλαιὸν Σαόννησον καλουμένην...ἐσχήκασι δὲ παλαιὰν
ἰδίαν διάλεκτον οἱ αὐτόχθονες ἧς πολλὰ ἐν ταῖς θυσίαις μέχρι τοῦ νῦν τηρεῖται...ὅρους
θέσθαι τῆς σωτηρίας.

[6] Hesych. *s.v.* ἐκ Μελίτης μαστιγίας, καλεῖται δὲ ὁ ἐν Μελίτῃ Ἡρακλῆς ἀλεξίκακος.
The Greek was doubtless, as Lewy points out, simply the translation of some such
Semitic divine title as מְמַלֵּט מֵרָעָה mᵉmallēṭ mērāʻā, Preserver-from-Evil.

an immigrant. Diodorus[1] records that while the Thebans and
others did honour to Herakles as a hero 'the Athenians were the
first to offer sacrifices to him as a god'; their pious example
influenced, he says, first the rest of Greece and afterwards the
whole habitable world. Strabo[2] hits the mark when he says 'as
in other matters the Athenians were hospitable in what concerned
the gods.'

Herakles in Melite was then in all probability a stranger; as
to Herakles in Diomeia there is no shadow of doubt. Plutarch[3]
begins his life of Themistocles with a story that shows in striking
fashion the limits of the hospitality extended to Herakles as the
typical stranger. 'The origin of Themistokles was too obscure to
be a source of distinction.' On his father's side he was an Athenian,
but on his mother's some said a Thracian, but Phanias stated
that she was a Karian, and Neanthes that she belonged to
Halikarnassos. Anyhow he was what the Athenians accounted
base-born ($\nu\acute{o}\theta o\varsigma$). 'The base-born youths subscribed to the
"Kynosarges," the gymnasium of Herakles, outside the city gates,
for Herakles, too, was not a true-born god but was introduced
by adoption inasmuch as his mother was a mortal. Accordingly,
Themistocles persuaded certain of the true-born youths to go to
Kynosarges and exercise there with him.' Kynosarges, haunt of
the base-born, outside the gates; there could be no better evidence
that its patron, Herakles, was a foreigner[4].

Themistocles has yet more evidence to yield us, and that of a
curious character. Themistocles, it will be remembered (p. 144),
had a home in Melite close to the barathron. Near to his home
he founded a sanctuary of Artemis 'to whom he gave the title of
Aristoboule[5].' This was among the many ways in which he annoyed

[1] Diod. iv. 39. Diodorus goes on to describe the strange primitive ceremony
of adoption by which Hera naturalized Herakles among the Olympians; see my
Proleg., p. 347.
[2] Strabo x. 471.
[3] Plut. *Vit. Them.* 1.
[4] The cult of Herakles in Diomeia contains other elements obviously Semitic, the
discussion of which would lead us far. The details are given in my *Myth. and Mon.
Ancient Athens*, p. 216, but the Semitic character of the 'white dog' legend I did not
then realize. Prof. Robertson Smith long ago (*Religion of the Semites*, p. 274, note 2),
pointed out that the supposed 'white dog' is really the 'dogs' enclosure' and that the
sacred dogs are a class of Semitic temple-ministrants (see Deut. xxiii. 18, and *C.I.S.*
No. 86). To the whole question of the Semitic elements in the worship of Herakles
I hope to return on another occasion.
[5] Plut. *Vit. Them.* 22...$\mathring{\eta}\nu$ '$A\rho\iota\sigma\tau o\beta o\acute{u}\lambda\eta\nu$ $\mu\grave{e}\nu$ $\pi\rho o\sigma\eta\gamma\acute{o}\rho\epsilon\upsilon\sigma\epsilon\nu$.

the Athenians. The cause of the annoyance, Plutarch thinks, was that he gave the title to commemorate his good advice before the battle of Salamis. But was this the real reason? Surely the dedication gave all glory to the goddess, not to himself? It is a curious and, I think, significant fact that we know of another Aristoboule, and she is a manifestly Semitic goddess. Porphyry, in enumerating instances of human sacrifice, says[1] that in Rhodes *on the 6th day of the month Metageitnion*, a man used to be sacrificed to Kronos. The custom, which had obtained for a long time, had been modified. A condemned criminal was kept alive till the feast of Kronos, and at the time of the feast they led the man outside the city gates opposite the image of Aristoboule, gave him wine to drink and slew him. If Themistocles was trying 'craftily,' as Plutarch[2] says, to affiliate a base-born to a true-born divinity, an Aristoboule to an Artemis, small wonder if the Athenians were annoyed. Perhaps the 'Karian' mother counted for something in the attempt.

The festival of Aristoboule in Rhodes, the grim Semitic Kronia, fell—and the fact is surely significant—in the month Metageitnion. Certain Herakleia, probably, though not quite certainly[3], the Herakleia in Kynosarges, fell in the same month; and of course the actual ceremonial of the Metageitnia mentioned by Plutarch. To this Metageitnia we now return. We have seen that the population of Melite, the worshippers of Herakles[4], were probably foreigners, and that at one time there

---

[1] Porphyr. *de Abst.* ii. 54 ἐθύετο γὰρ καὶ ἐν ῾Ρόδῳ μηνὶ Μεταγειτνιῶνι ἑκτῇ ἱσταμένου ἄνθρωπος τῷ Κρόνῳ ὃ δὴ ἐπὶ πολὺ κρατῆσαν ἔθος μετεβλήθη· ἕνα γὰρ τῶν ἐπὶ θανάτῳ δημοσίᾳ κατακριθέντων μέχρι μὲν τῶν Κρονίων συνεῖχον, ἐνστάσης δὲ τῆς ἑορτῆς προαγαγόντες τὸν ἄνθρωπον ἔξω πυλῶν ἄντικρυ τοῦ ᾿Αριστοβούλης ἔδους οἴνου ποτίσαντες ἔσφαττον. In this connection it is strange that the tradition of human sacrifice before the battle of Salamis, possibly apocryphal, attaches itself to Themistocles; see my *Prolegomena*, p. 489.

[2] Plut. *Vit. Them.* 1.

[3] Aug. Mommsen, *Feste der Stadt Athen*, p. 160. Probably Mommsen is right in his conjecture that the sacrifice of the Metageitnia mentioned by Plutarch was an actual part or at least preliminary to the *Herakleia*.

[4] I selected the worship of Herakles for discussion because we have definite evidence that Herakles is connected with Diomeia as well as Melite. An equally striking case of the shift of a foreign cult from Melite to the district of the Ilissos is that of Aphrodite Ourania. Pausanias (i. 14. 7) saw the sanctuary in Melite, noted its oriental origin and the current story that Porphyrion founded a sanctuary of Aphrodite in the deme Athimoneus, *i.e.* on the way from Marathon. When he came

was a shift of these Herakles worshippers from Melite to Diomeia. Is it not possible that the two facts are connected ? Plutarch leaves us in mid-air as to the time and cause of the *metastasis*, but be it observed the shift is from Melite, a district outside the old burgh, to Diomeia, a district, at least in part, outside the new. May it not have been felt when the new circuit-wall of Themistocles was complete that it comprised too many foreigners? If the shift took place soon after the building of the new fortifications the event would still be remembered at the performance (406 B.C.) of the *Frogs.*

At whatever date the *metastasis* took place thus much is clear. It was no chance incidental flitting of a few scattered families, but a substantial shift of population, and it adequately accounts for the curious duplication of sanctuaries. The foreign character of one element in that population and of the cult they carried with them has been emphasized because it provides at least a possible explanation of the shift, but it must not for a moment be supposed that all the sanctuaries and sanctities were necessarily foreign. We may conclude this portion of the evidence by noting an instance of mythological duplication specially convincing because wholly incidental and undesigned, the legend of Boreas and Oreithyia.

Pausanias[1] tells us that 'the Ilissus is the river where Oreithyia is said to have been playing when she was carried off by Boreas the North wind.' We are a little surprised; what was the king's daughter doing playing down by the Ilissus far from her father's citadel, and was not the Ilissus rather a sheltered spot for the North wind ? Plato[2] in the *Phaedrus*, as Sokrates and Phaedrus are lying under the 'tallest plane tree' on the bank of the Ilissus, makes Phaedrus say 'I should like to know whether the place is not somewhere here where Boreas is said to have carried off Oreithyia; Sokrates says it is not far, about a quarter of a mile off, and that there is some sort of an

to the Ilissos to the district of the Gardens (i. 19. 2) he sees the sanctuary of Aphrodite Ourania, her image as a *herm* and the inscription says she is eldest of the Fates. He notes that there is 'no local legend.' How should there be if the cult was transplanted? From this sanctuary he passes on next to Kynosarges.

[1] Paus. i. 19. 5.   [2] Plat. *Phaedr.* 229 A.

altar there—and adds 'there is a discrepancy however about the spot; according to another version of the story she was taken from the Areopagos and not from this place.'

We pass to our fourth source of error.

4. *Confusion as to Kallirrhoë and Enneakrounos.*

Misunderstanding as regards the duplicated sanctuaries was explicable, even natural, but the downward road once embarked on leads to a deeper depth. Those who believe that Thucydides is concerned to prove that the ancient city lay Southwards have to find for the Fair-Fount and Nine-Spouts of Thucydides a home other than the rock of the Pnyx; they place the ancient city well, whence the king's daughters drew their water, outside, not only of the walls of Themistocles, but even of the later and wider enclosure of Hadrian; they place it on the Ilissus, at a distance of over half-a-mile as the crow flies from the citadel gate. If the king's daughters really ventured out there we must not, considering the convention of the times, too severely blame the attacks of the rude Pelasgians. And assuredly, if any one will try the experiment of carrying a bucket of water from Kallirrhoë on the Ilissus to the top of the Acropolis on a hot summer's day, he will imagine those king's daughters as cast in more than mortal mould.

In the days when the Kallirrhoë of Thucydides could be placed on the Ilissus the conception of Athens formed by scholars was of an Athens in the days of Pericles. To speak of ancient Athens as a 'Mycenaean' city would then have been unmeaning, if not positively insulting. As soon as we realise the conditions of a Pelasgian burgh, with its king and his immediate dependents massed upon and close up to the citadel, we know that the citadel-well *must* be close at hand—the Fair-Fount of the Pnyx is already full far.

As to the Fair-Fount (Kallirrhoë) on the Ilissus, there has been and still prevails much confusion. A Kallirrhoë there certainly *is* on the Ilissus; the women of Athens wash their clothes there to-day[1],

---

[1] See *Myth. and Mon. Anc. Athens*, p. 226 and Fig. 17. Since I wrote that account excavations have been undertaken by the Greek Archaeological Society on the supposed site of the Enneakrounos on the Ilissus; traces of channels for the conducting of water have been found, but the water so conducted is not drinkable. For report see Πρακτικὰ τῆς Ἀρχ. Ἐταιρίας, 1893, pp. 111—136.

and the existence of this Kallirrhoë Prof. Dörpfeld has never denied. Nay, he expressly points out that even in the days of Thucydides the Kallirrhoë of the Pnyx had already lost its name, and needs to be recalled to his readers. If, as has been seen, many sanctuaries were transferred and names duplicated there is nothing (1) impossible nor (2) injurious to our theory, if the new Kallirrhoë was sometimes, like its old archetype, called Enneakrounos. Though as a matter of fact this seems not to have been the case.

Two ancient authorities, and two only, appear at first sight definitely to place the Enneakrounos on the Ilissus. These must be examined in detail. First, the *Etymologicum Magnum*[1], under the heading *Enneakrounos*, says, 'a fountain at Athens by the Ilissus, which was formerly Kallirrhoë, to which they go to fetch the water for baths for brides.' Unquestionably, whoever wrote this thought the Enneakrounos was on the Ilissus. But then by the time the *Etymologicum Magnum* was compiled the old Kallirrhoë at the Pnyx was long forgotten. The statement looks as if it had come originally from Thucydides[2], and as if the topographical 'by the Ilissus' had been added by some ambitious but ignorant compiler.

Against this statement of the *Etymologicum Magnum*, for what it is worth, we may set the statement of another lexicographer[3]. Explaining the expression 'Wedding Baths,' he says, 'the baths brought from a fountain from the agora.' The wildest topographer has never placed the agora by the Ilissus, though it might go there with quite as good reason as the ancient city well.

A second ancient literary authority seems at first sight indisputably to place the Enneakrounos near to the temple of Zeus Olympios and, if there, then, as a necessary consequence, on the

---

[1] *Etym. Mag.* Ἐννεάκρουνος· κρήνη Ἀθήνησι παρὰ τὸν Ἴλισσον, ἡ πρότερον Καλλιρόη ἔσκεν ἀφ' ἧς τὰ λουτρὰ ταῖς γαμουμέναις μετίασι. Πολύζηλος Δημοτυνδαρέῳ

'ἕξει πρὸς Ἐννεάκρουνον, εὔυδρον τόπον.'

See Koch, *Frag. Com.* vol. I. pp. 790—2. Polyzelos is of course not responsible for the statement about the Ilissos.

[2] Hesych. *s.v.* Ἐννεάκρουνος takes his account and acknowledges it ὥς φησι καὶ Θουκυδίδης.

[3] Suidas, *s.v.* νυμφικὰ λουτρά—τὰ εἰς γάμους ἐκ τῆς ἀγορᾶς ἀπὸ κρήνης λαμβανόμενα.

Ilissus. In the preface to a treatise by Hierocles[1] on *Veterinary Medicine* there occurs, apropos of the age to which horses and mules live, the following statement : ' Tarantinos narrates that the Athenians *when they were building the temple of Zeus near Enneakrounos* passed a decree that all the beasts of burden should be driven in from Attica to the town.' This seems perfectly definite and circumstantial, and the passage has been eagerly seized on by all those who wished to prove that the Enneakrounos was on the Ilissus. Quite naturally, but wait a moment. It is essential that the passage be read to the end. Tarantinos goes on, ' and a certain husbandman through fear of this decree drove in an aged mule in its eightieth year. But the people out of respect for its age enacted that the mule was to be leader of all the beasts of burden employed in the building of the temple, it was to walk in front unyoked and unspurred, and that none of the wheat-merchants or barley-merchants were to drive it away from their houses or prevent it from browsing.'

The aged mule story is charming ; we can scarcely hear it too often, but somehow it *is* oddly familiar ; have we not heard it before in slightly different form ? Yes ; surely it is the story Plutarch[2] tells when he is recounting the kindness of Cato to his beasts. ' A good man will take care of his horses and dogs, not only while they are young, but when they are old and past service. Thus the people of Athens, *when they were building the Hecatompedon* set at liberty those mules which they thought had worked hardest and let them go free, and one of them, it is said, afterwards came of her own accord back to the works and trotted by the side of the beasts who were drawing the waggons and led them on and seemed to be exhorting and encouraging them. And the people passed a vote that she should be entertained at

[1] Hierocles, *Hippiatr. praef.* sub fin. Ταραντῖνος δὲ ἱστορεῖ τὸν τοῦ Διὸς νεὼν κατασκευάζοντας 'Αθηναίους 'Εννεακρούνου πλησίον εἰσελαθῆναι ψηφίσασθαι τὰ ἐκ τῆς 'Αττικῆς εἰς τὸ ἄστυ ζεύγη ἄπαντα· φόβῳ δὲ τοῦ ψηφίσματός τινα τῶν γεωργῶν ἡμίονον ἀγαγεῖν γέραιον ἄγοντα ἔτος ὀγδοηκοστόν, τὸν δὲ δῆμον τιμῇ τοῦ γήρως προηγητόρα τῶν ζεύγων εἰς τὴν κατασκευὴν αὐτὸν τοῦ νεὼ καταστῆσαι προβαδίζειν τε ἄζευκτον καὶ ἄπληκτον ψηφίσασθαι μηδένα δὲ τῶν πυροπώλων ἢ κριθοπώλων ἀπελαύνειν αὐτὸν τῆς ἐστίας ἢ ἀπείργειν τῆς βρώσεως. It will be seen that I have construed πλησίον with κατασκευάζοντας, that being the usual rendering. Dyer has however pointed out (*Journal of Philology*, III. 1871, p. 90) that it might be taken with εἰσελαθῆναι.

[2] Plut. *Cat.* v. ὁ δὲ τῶν 'Αθηναίων δῆμος οἰκοδομῶν τὸν 'Εκατόμπεδον, and *De sollert. an.* XIII. τὸν γὰρ ἑκατόμπεδον νεὼν Περικλέους ἐν ἀκροπόλει.

the public expense to the day of her death.' The same story is told by Aelian[1] of the time '*when the Athenians were building the Parthenon,*' and he quotes as his authority Aristotle. It is Aristotle[2] who has set the whole uncertainty going. He tells the story of the time 'when at Athens *they were building the temple.*'

By the 'temple' Aelian and Plutarch are almost certainly right in understanding the Parthenon. If they are right, we can infer that Tarantinos, an author whose date is unknown, and whom we have no ground for regarding as an authority on Athenian topography, has made at any rate one mistake, when he identifies 'the temple' with the great temple of his own day, the temple 'of Zeus.' Tarantinos is, presumably, taking the story from Aristotle. If so, it is clear that, besides wrongly identifying 'the temple,' he supposed that the Enneakrounos, which on this hypothesis he for the first time imports into the story, was identical with the Kallirrhoë of the Ilissos[3]. But what is the value of his evidence? His supporters may fairly be challenged to produce the credentials of a witness whose only title to be regarded as an authority is an identification almost certainly wrong. There is nothing to rebut the simple supposition that, like the author of the *Etymologicum Magnum,* he is merely confusing the two Kallirrhoës[4].

---

[1] Ael. *Hist. An.* VI. 49 Ἡνίκα γοῦν Ἀθηναῖοι κατεσκεύαζον τὸν Παρθενῶνα.

[2] Aristot. *Hist. An.* VI. 24 ἤδη γάρ τις βεβίωκεν ἔτη καὶ ὀγδοήκοντα οἷον Ἀθήνησιν ὅτε τὸν νεὼν ᾠκοδόμουν· ὃς καὶ ἀφειμένος ἤδη διὰ τὸ γῆρας, συναμπρεύων καὶ παραπορευόμενος παρώξυνε πρὸς τὸ ἔργον ὡς ἐψηφίσαντο μὴ ἀπελαύνειν αὐτὸν τοὺς σιτοπώλους ἀπὸ τῶν τηλιῶν. Aristotle is obviously the ultimate source of the statement of Tarantinos.

[3] Professor Ernest Gardner in his *Ancient Athens,* p. 20, quotes the passage of Tarantinos as part of the 'overwhelming evidence that Kallirrhoë lay in the bed of Ilissus.' No one, so far as I know, has ever doubted that there was *a* Kallirrhoë in the bed of the Ilissus, the point is whether the particular Kallirrhoë which was transformed into Enneakrounos lay there. Attention was I believe first drawn by Prof. Dörpfeld to the various temple buildings with which the mule-story is connected. I owe the references to Dr Bodensteiner's 'Enneakrounos und Lenaion,' *Blätter f. das Gym. Schulwesen,* 1895, p. 31.

[4] It is almost incredible that the fact that Alciphron in one epistle (III. 49. 1) mentions Enneakrounos—as a source of ordinary drinking water—and in another (III. 51. 1) speaks of Kallirrhoë—as an object of sentiment—has been urged as an argument for an Enneakrounos on the Ilissos. He is obviously speaking of two different springs. Pliny (*N. H.* IV. 7. 11) enumerating the Attic fountains says 'Cephisia Larine Calliroe, Enneacrunos,' and some editors assume that Pliny wrote Calliroe Enneacrunos by apposition. Surely, as Dyer observes (*Journ. Phil.* III. p. 87), since Pliny was reckoning up the actual number of fountains, he would have given his readers notice that these were only two different names for the same object, and have inserted *seu* or some such word between them.

Finally, supposing for a moment that the passage of Thucydides leaves us in doubt as to the site of the Enneakrounos, naturally our next step would be to ask what does our next best authority, Pausanias, say ? Pausanias is a topographer by profession, surely we shall learn from him where he saw the well-house. Pausanias[1] after seeing the statues of Harmodios and Aristogeiton 'not far from' the temple of Ares, passes straight on to a small group of monuments which he links together more or less clearly; they are the Odeion; near to it the Enneakrounos; above or beyond this the temples of Demeter and Kore; a little further on the temple of Eukleia. It is quite true that he links the Odeion by no connecting particle, but that is his frequent practice when passing straight from one monument to another.

The uninstructed reader in his simplicity would naturally think that, as Pausanias passes straight from the statues of the Tyrant Slayers to the Odeion, the two lay somewhere not far apart, and so they did. The Odeion in the days of Pausanias would almost certainly be near the site of the ancient orchestra, where still are faint remains of a semi-circular building (Fig. 46). Anyhow it stood close to the Areopagos. But this is too simple and natural. Pausanias we are told, here and nowhere else, abruptly breaks his narrative of the buildings in the Kerameikos, and with no apparent reason and no hint in the text, flies off for nearly half-a-mile and plants his reader on the banks of the Ilissus,—a district, be it noted, that he later describes in detail,— whence he shortly returns again without warning and finishes his account of the Kerameikos. In a word we are presented with what is known as the 'Enneakrounos Episode.' Various causes are suggested for the 'Episode'; the leaves of the MS. got mixed, or Pausanias was staying with friends near the Ilissus, and went home to lunch. The real cause of the 'Episode' is that Thucydides has been misunderstood, and that the late compiler of the *Etymologicum Magnum* has blundered. Pausanias[2] saw the Odeion in the neighbourhood of the old orchestra at the south-

---

[1] Paus. I. 8. 5 οὐ πόρρω δὲ ἑστᾶσιν Ἁρμόδιος καὶ Ἀριστογείτων. I. 14. 1 ἐς δὲ τὸ Ἀθήνῃσιν ἐσελθοῦσιν Ὠδεῖον...πλησίον δέ ἐστι κρήνη, καλοῦσι δὲ αὐτὴν Ἐννεάκρουνον... ναοὶ δὲ ὑπὲρ τὴν κρήνην ἔτι δὲ ἀπωτέρω ναὸς Εὐκλείας.

[2] For further evidence on these sanctuaries, see my *Myth. and Mon. Anc. Athens*, pp. 89—111.

west of the Areopagos, the Enneakrounos near to it by the Pnyx rock, the temples of Demeter and Kore 'above it' *on* the Pnyx rock where were the Thesmophorion[1] and the temple of Eukleia 'not far off'; his course of sight-seeing was here as elsewhere orderly and undisturbed.

Pausanias is seen to be at one with Thucydides and, thanks to Prof. Dörpfeld, the evidence of both has been confirmed by excavation; the sources of error and confusion in late authors, lexicographers and modern archaeologists have come to light. Surely now at last the 'Enneakrounos Episode' may be laid to sleep in peace.

[1] For the Eleusinion and Thesmophorion, see Dörpfeld, *A. Mitt.* xxii. 1897, p. 477, and 1896, p. 106.

CRITICAL NOTE

On Thucydides II. 15 §§ 3—6. For text see p. 7.

It seems to me that there is probably no corruption at all in this passage and that we may follow the MSS. throughout. (The MSS. are Hude's A B C E F G M.)

l. 1. πρὸ τούτου : πρὸ τοῦ C G. No improvement, being a little less definite than πρὸ τούτου ; but on technical grounds quite likely to be right.

ἡ ἀκρόπολις ἡ νῦν οὖσα πόλις ἦν : Hude transposes ἡ, so as to read ἡ ἀκρόπολις νῦν οὖσα ἡ πόλις ἦν. Perhaps slightly easier. Stuart Jones keeps the MS. reading.

l. 2. καὶ ἄλλων θεῶν ἐστι : Classen marked a lacuna here, and most editors follow him. The meaning of ἄλλων is undoubtedly 'other than Athena,' to whom in Thucydides' time the Acropolis belonged. The question is whether in order to make ἄλλων clear, Thucydides must have mentioned Athena in this clause ; or whether from (1) the mention of τῇ θεῷ in the last sentence, and (2) the obvious and close connexion between Athena and the Acropolis of Athens, the reference to her could be 'understood.'

On purely critical grounds this is hard to decide, as it depends on various unsolved problems about the condition of our Thucydides MSS., and the degree of divergence from smooth writing of which Thucydides was capable. But, if we do suppose that a line has fallen out, I do not think the argument quite suits with corrections like Classen's ἄλλων θεῶν ἐστι <καὶ τὰ τῆς 'Αθηνᾶς>, or Wilamowitz's ἐν αὐτῇ τῇ ἀκροπόλει <καὶ ὑπ' αὐτῇ τῆς τ' 'Αθηναίας> καὶ ἄλλων θεῶν. Everyone knew that Athena lived on the Acropolis. You would need <οὐ μόνον τῆς 'Αθηναίας ἀλλὰ> καὶ. And this sense, after all, is just what we have from the text as it stands.

l. 4. τὸ ἐν Λίμναις Διονύσου : τὸ <τοῦ> Cobet : on purely linguistic grounds, of which it is hard to estimate the cogency. The same remark applies to the proposed omissions of either τῇ δωδεκάτῃ or of ἐν μηνὶ 'Ανθεστηριῶνι in the next sentence.

l. 7. σκευασάντων : κελευσάντων two MSS. (C G), clearly wrong.

l. 8. ἐκείνη MSS.: ἐκεῖνοι (i.e. οἱ ἀρχαῖοι) Bekker. This makes the construction easier, and is palaeographically very probable.

τὰ πλείστου ἄξια : τὰ πλεῖστα ἄξια two MSS. (A B): a mere slip.

G. M.

BIBLIOGRAPHY.

THUCYDIDES, II. 15, discussion of.

N. Wecklein, *Sitzungsber. der Bayer. Akad.*, 97, 1887.

P. Stahl, "Thukydides über das alte Athen vor Theseus." *Rhein. Mus. für Philol.*, L. p. 566, 1895.

W. Dörpfeld, "Das alte Athen vor Theseus." *Rhein. Mus. für Philol.*, LI. p. 127, 1896.

C. Wachsmuth, "Neue Beiträge zur Topographie von Athen. Das Thukydideische Ur-Athen." *Abhandl. der K. Sächs. Ges. der Wiss.*, XLI. 1899

A. W. Verrall, "Thucydides II. 15 and Recent Explorations." *Classical Review*, XIV. p. 274, 1900.

L. R. Farnell, "Questions concerning Attic Topography and Religion." *Classical Review*, p. 369, 1900.

M. Carroll, "Thucydides, Pausanias and the Dionysium in Limnis." *Classical Review*, XIX. p. 325, 1905.

PAUSANIAS, Commentaries on.

T. H. Dyer, *Ancient Athens, its History, Topography and Remains*, ch. vi. p. 180 sqq., 1873.

Harrison and Verrall, *Mythology and Monuments of Ancient Athens*, p. 90, 1890.

O. Fallis, *Pausanias auf der Agora von Athen.* Munich, 1895.

Hitzig und Blümner, *Pausaniae Graeciae Descriptio*, 1896.

J. G. Frazer, *Pausanias' Description of Greece*, 1898.

Official Reports of Excavations by the German Archaeological Institute at Athens published in—

(1) *Mittheilungen des K. Deutschen Archaeologischen Instituts in Athen.*

(*a*)   Die Ausgrabungen am Westabhange der Acropolis.

I.   W. Dörpfeld, "Allgemeine Uebersicht," XIX. p. 496, Pl. XIV., 1894.

II.   W. Dörpfeld, "Das Lenaion oder Dionysion in den Limnai," XX. p. 161, Pl. IV., 1895.

III.   H. Schrader, "Funde im Gebiete des Dionysion," XXI. p. 265, Pl. VIII.—X., 1896.

IV.   O. Körte, "Das Heiligtum des Amynos," XXI. p. 287, Pl. XI., 1896 ; and see Körte, "Bezirk eines Heilgottes," XVIII. p. 231, Pl. XI., 1893.

V.   C. Watzinger, "Einzelfunde," XXVI. p. 305, 1901.

(*b*) Die Ausgrabungen an der Enneakrounos.

I. W. Dörpfeld, XVII. p. 439, 1892.

II. W. Dörpfeld, XIX. p. 143, 1894 ;

and see Dörpfeld, "Die verschiedenen Odeien in Athen," XVII. p. 252, 1892.

S. Wide, "Inschrift der Iobakchen," XIX. p. 248, 1894.

H v. Prott, "Enneakrunos, Lenaion, u. Διονύσιον ἐν Λίμναις," XXIII. p. 205, 1898 ; and see Prott, Nachtrag dazu, XXIII. p. 367, 1898.

C. Watzinger, "Mimologen. Terracotta vom Westabhange," XXVI. p. 1, Pl. I., 1901.

C. Watzinger, "Vasenfunde aus Athen," XXVI. p. 50, Pl. II.—IV., 1901.

Fr. Gräber, "Die Enneakrunos," XXX. p. 58, 1905.

E. Ziller, "Wasserleitungen von Athen," II. 1877.

Fabricius, "Polykrates at Samos," IX. p. 165, 1884.

Delbrück u. K. G. Vollmöller, "Das Brunnenhaus des Theagenes," XXV. p. 23, Pl. VII., VIII., 1900.

Funde.

1. "Aphrodite Pandemos," XIV. p. 121, 1889 ; and see G. Kawerau u. F. Weibach, "Die Pandemosweihung auf der Akropolis," XXX. p. 298, 1905.

2. Discoveries, various, XV. p. 343, 444, 1890 ; XVI. pp. 140, 252, 361, 443, 1891 ; XVII. pp. 90, 281, 449, 1892.

3. "Stoa Basileios," XXI. pp. 103, 458, 1896 ; XXII. pp. 225, 476, 1897.

Sitzungsprotokolle.

W. Dörpfeld, "Alopeke," XX. p. 507, 1895.

P. Wolters, "Δεξίων," XX. p. 508, 1895.

W. Dörpfeld, "Enneakrunos im Siebzehnten Jahrhundert" (Guillet et Coronelli), XX. p. 510, 1895.

W. Dörpfeld, "Aphrodite Pandemos," XX. p. 511, 1895.

(2) *Antike Denkmäler d. K. Deutschen Archäologischen Instituts Berlin.* (Official plans of Excavations with Text.) Ausgrabungen in Athen, 1899—1901, II., Pl. 37, 38.

(3) *Jahrbuch d. K. D. Arch. Inst.*

W. Dörpfeld, "Anzeiger," XI. p. 19, 1896.

C. Belger, "Anzeiger," XI. p. 40, 1896.

H. 11

Topography of Athens:
General.

M. Leake, *Topography of Athens*, 1821.

M. Leake, *Topography of Athens and the Demi*, 1841.

P. Forchhammer, "Topographie von Athen" (*Kieler Philol. Studien*). Kiel, 1841.

E. Curtius, "Attische Studien" (*Abhandl. d. Göttinger Ges. d. Wiss.* XI. XII.) Göttingen, I. 1862 ; II. 1865.

E. Curtius, *Erläuternder Text der Sieben Karten zur Topographie von Athen*. Berlin, 1868.

H. G. Lolling, *K. Baedekers Griechenland*, pp. 34—83, 1883.

H. G. Lolling, "Anhang zur Hellenischen Landeskunde und Topographie" (I. Müller's *Handb. d. C. A. W.*), III. 290.

A. Milchhöfer, "Athen" (Baumeister, *Denkmäler des class. Alt.*, I. p. 144, 1884).

C. Wachsmuth, *Die Stadt Athen im Alterthum*, I. 1874, II. 1890.

C. Wachsmuth, "Neue Beiträge zur Topog. von Athen" (*Abh. d. K. S. Ges. d. Wiss.*, XLI.).

W. Judeich, "Anzeiger von C. Wachsmuth, Stadt Athen," *Jahrbuch für Class. Phil.* v. A. Fleckeisen, p. 721, 1890.

Pickard, "Dionysos ἐν Λίμναις." *Am. J. of Arch.* VIII. p. 56, 1893.

J. Middleton, Plans and drawings of Athenian Buildings, *J.H.S.* Supplement III., 1900.

A. Malinin, "Zwei Streitfragen der Topographie v. Athen," 1901.

O. Jahn and A. Michaelis, *Arx Athenarum a Pausania Descripta*, 1901.

A. Michaelis, *Tabulae Arcem Athenarum illustrantes*, 1901.

E. A. Gardner, *Ancient Athens*, 1902.

H. Lechat, *Au Musée de l'Acropole d'Athènes*, 1902.

H. Lechat, *La Sculpture Attique avant Phidias*, 1904.

C. H. Weller, "The pre-Periclean Propylaea on the Acropolis of Athens," *Am. Journ. Arch.*, pp. 33—70, Pl. I.—VI., 1904.

Pan's Cave.

W. Dörpfeld, Report, *Ath. Mitth.* XXI. p. 460, 1897.

P. Kabbadias, Τοπογραφικὰ 'Αθηνῶν, *Ephem. Arch.* XXI. Pl. I.—IV. pp. 1—32, 1897.

Bulletin de Corr. Hel. XX. p. 382.

A. Michaelis, *op. cit.*, *Atlas*, Pl. XVII., 1, XVI., 1 *a*.

Pelargikon.

H. Unger, "Enneakrunos und Pelasgikon," p. 263 (*Sitzungsber. d. K. Bayer. Akad. d. Wiss. zu München*), 1874.

W. Miller, "A History of the Acropolis of Athens." *Amer. Journ. Arch.* VIII. p. 481, 1893.

J. W. White, Περὶ τοῦ Πελαργικοῦ ἐπὶ Περικλέους. 'Εφημερὶς 'Αρχαιολογική, 1894, p. 2.

G. Nikolaïdes, Περὶ Καλλιρρόης καὶ 'Εννεακρούνου. *Eph. Arch.* 1893, p. 176.

W. Dörpfeld, 'Η 'Εννεάκρουνος καὶ ἡ Καλλιρρόη. *Eph. Arch.* 1894, p. 1.

Enneakrounos.

A complete list of the scattered and voluminous foreign literature of the " Enneakrounos Episode " is not given here, because full references will be found in three books which must necessarily be in the hands of any one attempting an independent examination of this or any other question relating to the topography of Athens— these are :

1. H. Hitzig and H. Blümner, *Pausaniae Graeciae Descriptio*, Berlin, 1896 (for the Enneakrounos episode, I. part 1, pp. 166—172 and pp. 187—191).

2. C. Wachsmuth, "Athenai," in Pauly-Wissowa, *Real-Encyclopädie.* Supplement, Erstes Heft, Stuttgart, 1903.

3. W. Judeich, *Topographie von Athen*, München, 1905, in Iwan von Müller's *Handbuch d. kl. Altertumswissenschaft*, Band 3, Abt. 2, Hälfte 2.

The classical sources for the *Enneakrounos* and other topographical questions are conveniently collected by Dr Milchhoefer in E. Curtius, *Die Stadtgeschichte von Athen*, Berlin, 1891.

INDEX.

CLASSICAL AUTHORS.

For EU product safety concerns, contact us at Calle de José Abascal, 56–1°, 28003 Madrid, Spain or eugpsr@cambridge.org.

www.ingramcontent.com/pod-product-compliance
Ingram Content Group UK Ltd.
Pitfield, Milton Keynes, MK11 3LW, UK
UKHW012342130625
459647UK00009B/483